Programming Windows Workflow Foundation: Practical WF Techniques and Examples using XAML and C#

A C# developer's guide to the features and programming interfaces of Windows Workflow Foundation

K. Scott Allen

BIRMINGHAM - MUMBAI

Programming Windows Workflow Foundation: Practical WF Techniques and Examples using XAML and C#

First published: December 2006

Production Reference: 1121206

Published by Packt Publishing Ltd.
32 Lincoln Road
Olton
Birmingham, B27 6PA, UK.

ISBN 1-904811-21-3

www.packtpub.com

Cover Image by www.visionwt.com

Credits

Author

K. Scott Allen

Reviewer

Dan Kahler

Development Editor

Douglas Paterson

Assistant Development Editor

Nikhil Bangera

Technical Editor

Viraj Joshi

Editorial Manager

Dipali Chittar

Project Manager

Patricia Weir

Project Coordinator

Abhijeet Deobhakta

Indexer

Bhushan Pangaonkar

Proofreader

Chris Smith

Layouts and Illustrations

Shantanu Zagade

Cover Designer

Shantanu Zagade

About the Author

Scott Allen is a software architect with 14 years of experience in commercial software development. Scott has worked on platforms ranging from 8-bit embedded systems to highly scalable and distributed web applications. For the last six years, Scott has concentrated on the .NET platform, and is a Microsoft MVP. Scott presents at local code camps and national conferences.

Scott is a founder of the website OdeToCode.com, where he publishes articles and maintains a blog. Scott previously coauthored *Building Websites with the ASP.NET Community Starter Kit* for Packt Publishing, and has also published articles in *MSDN Magazine* and *Dr. Dobb's Journal*.

I'd like to thank Packt's Douglas Paterson for putting up with my antics over the years. I'd also like to acknowledge the rest of the Packt team, including Patricia Weir, Abhijeet Deobhakta, and Viraj Joshi, for their efforts.

Dan Kahler and Nikhil Bangera made this a better book with their diligent reviewing efforts, and I am grateful.

Finally, there is Beaker. While I was writing, and the rest of the world was sleeping, Beaker would be on my desk or curled next to my feet. She'd be sleeping too, but she was always close by until she passed away. I miss you, Beaker.

About the Reviewer

Dan Kahler is a Senior Engineer with Verizon Business. With over eight years of experience developing and administering Windows and Web-based solutions, he specializes in using Microsoft technologies to simplify and automate day-to-day system administration tasks and to integrate line-of-business applications. Dan previously contributed to the *Microsoft Log Parser Toolkit* (Syngress, ISBN: 1-932266-52-6) as a contributing author, and contributed to the *Microsoft Internet Information Services (IIS) 6.0 Resource Kit* (Microsoft Press, ISBN: 0-735614-20-2) as a technical reviewer and tester. He is active in the Baltimore .NET user group (www.baltomsdn.com). Dan currently resides in Eldersburg, Maryland with his wife Shannon and children Nicole and Ethan.

Table of Contents

Preface

Windows Workflow Foundation (WF) is a technology for defining, executing, and managing workflows. It is part of the .NET Framework 3.0 and will be available natively in the Windows Vista operating system.

Windows Workflow Foundation might be the most significant piece of middleware to arrive on the Windows platform since COM+ and the Distributed Transaction Coordinator. The difference is, not every application needs a distributed transaction, but nearly every application does have a workflow encoded inside.

This book will help you add that workflow power to your applications.

What This Book Covers

Chapter 1 introduces us to the concept of workflow and describes how Windows Workflow can solve the difficult problems inherent in workflow solutions. We'll become familiar with **activities** as the basic building blocks of a workflow definition and demonstrate how to author a simple workflow using Visual Studio 2005. This chapter also describes the runtime services available with WF. By the end of the chapter we will be able to identify the primary features of Windows Workflow.

Chapter 2 concentrates on authoring workflows. Specifically, we'll look at how to build workflows with C#, and with extensible application markup language (**XAML**). Looking at the workflow compiler, we'll have a better understanding of how WF uses code generation to produce classes from workflow markup, and how this generated code can combine with our hand-written code to produce a workflow type. This chapter will provide the fundamental knowledge needed to understand how WF operates during the compilation phase.

In *Chapter 3*, we will turn our attention to sequential workflows. We will examine the `SequenceActivity` and learn about the events fired by the workflow runtime during the life of a workflow instance. Using Visual Studio, we will build workflows that accept parameters and communicate with a host process by invoking methods and listening for events. The chapter concludes with a workflow example that raises an exception and uses a fault handler.

Chapter 4 examines each activity in the WF base activity library. We will look at the control flow activities, communication activities, and transaction-oriented activities. The chapter also examines web service activities, rule-centric activities, and state activities. The goal of this chapter is to make us aware of all the capabilities provided by the base activity library, with an eye towards understanding how each activity can solve a particular problem.

With an understanding of what is available in the base activity library, we can look at building our own custom activities in *Chapter 5*. This chapter examines the motivations for building custom activities, and provides examples of building a custom activity using both a compositional approach and a derivation approach. We'll see how to build a custom validator and designer for our activity, and also understand the advantages of using dependency properties. The chapter ends by covering the execution context, which we must understand to build robust activities.

Chapter 6 covers the workflow runtime, workflow diagnostics, and the out-of-the-box services provided for WF by Microsoft. The chapter demonstrates how to configure services both declaratively and programmatically. We'll see examples of how to use a scheduling service, persistence service, and tracking service. The chapter provides enough information to allow a developer to select and configure the services needed for a wide variety of scenarios and environments.

Chapter 7 focuses on building event-driven workflows using state machines. We'll see how WF models the traditional state machine using activities, and we will build a workflow to handle external events and react with state transitions. We'll also see how to track and examine the history of state machine execution. The chapter ends with an examination of a hierarchical state machine, which provides all the knowledge we need to tackle tough problems with event-driven workflows.

Chapter 8 is dedicated to workflow communications. The chapter explains how to use correlated local services for communication with a host process, and web service activities for communication across a network. By the end of the chapter we'll uncover the queuing service that is used behind the scenes of a workflow to coordinate and deliver messages.

Finally, *Chapter 9* is about rules and conditions in Windows Workflow. This discusses the role of business rules in software development and provides examples of how WF's rules engine can take away some of the burden of rule development. The chapter takes an in-depth look at rule execution in the `PolicyActivity`, and recording diagnostic information about rule evaluation. We'll come away with the knowledge we need to build rule-based solutions using Windows Workflow.

What You Need for This Book

Windows Workflow Foundation is one part of the .NET 3.0 framework. To run Windows Workflow, you'll need to download and install the .NET 3.0 redistributable (see the links below):

.NET 3.0 (x86): `http://go.microsoft.com/fwlink/?LinkID=70848`

.NET 3.0 (x64): `http://go.microsoft.com/fwlink/?LinkID=70849`

Visual Studio 2005 extensions for .NET Framework 3.0 (Windows Workflow Foundation):

`http://www.microsoft.com/downloads/details.aspx?FamilyId=`
`5D61409E-1FA3-48CF-8023-E8F38E709BA6&displaylang=en`

The .NET 3.0 runtime requires Windows Server 2003 SP1, Windows XP SP2, or Windows Vista. To develop Windows Workflow solutions you'll need to download the Visual Studio 2005 extensions for .NET Framework 3.0.

Conventions

In this book, you will find a number of styles of text that distinguish between different kinds of information. Here are some examples of these styles, and an explanation of their meaning.

There are three styles for code. Code words in text are shown as follows:

"The `codeActivity1_ExecuteCode` method is here and waiting for us to provide an implementation"

A block of code will be set as follows:

```
using System;
using System.Workflow.Activities;

namespace chapter2_library
{
  public sealed partial class PureCode: SequentialWorkflowActivity
  {
    public PureCode()
    {
      InitializeComponent();
    }

  }
```

```
    }
```

When we wish to draw your attention to a particular part of a code block, the
relevant lines or items will be made bold:

```
using System;
using System.Workflow.Activities;

namespace chapter2_library
{
  public sealed partial class PureCode: SequentialWorkflowActivity
  {
    public PureCode()
    {
      InitializeComponent();
    }
  }
}
```

New terms and **important words** are introduced in a bold-type font. Words that you
see on the screen, in menus or dialog boxes for example, appear in our text like this:
"Right-click the workflow and select the **Delete** option".

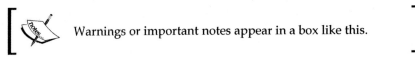

Warnings or important notes appear in a box like this.

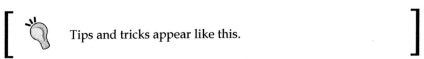

Tips and tricks appear like this.

Reader Feedback

Feedback from our readers is always welcome. Let us know what you think about
this book, what you liked or may have disliked. Reader feedback is important for us
to develop titles that you really get the most out of.

To send us general feedback, simply drop an email to feedback@packtpub.com,
making sure to mention the book title in the subject of your message.

If there is a book that you need and would like to see us publish, please send
us a note in the **SUGGEST A TITLE** form on www.packtpub.com or email
suggest@packtpub.com.

If there is a topic that you have expertise in and you are interested in either writing or contributing to a book, see our author guide on www.packtpub.com/authors.

Customer Support

Now that you are the proud owner of a Packt book, we have a number of things to help you to get the most from your purchase.

Downloading the Example Code for the Book

Visit http://www.packtpub.com/support, and select this book from the list of titles to download any example code or extra resources for this book. The files available for download will then be displayed.

The downloadable files contain instructions on how to use them.

Errata

Although we have taken every care to ensure the accuracy of our contents, mistakes do happen. If you find a mistake in one of our books—maybe a mistake in text or code—we would be grateful if you would report this to us. By doing this you can save other readers from frustration, and help to improve subsequent versions of this book. If you find any errata, report them by visiting http://www.packtpub.com/support, selecting your book, clicking on the **Submit Errata** link, and entering the details of your errata. Once your errata have been verified, your submission will be accepted and the errata added to the list of existing errata. The existing errata can be viewed by selecting your title from http://www.packtpub.com/support.

Questions

You can contact us at questions@packtpub.com if you are having a problem with some aspect of the book, and we will do our best to address it.

1
Hello, Workflow

…thoughts arrive like butterflies — Gossard / Vedder

Windows Workflow might be the most significant piece of middleware to arrive on the Windows platform since COM+ and the Distributed Transaction Coordinator. The difference is, not every application needs a distributed transaction, but nearly every application does have a workflow encoded inside. To understand the types of problems Windows Workflow is designed to solve, let's talk about workflow in a generic sense.

What is a workflow? A simple definition would say a workflow is the series of steps, decisions, and rules needed to complete a specific task. Think of the workflow that takes place when you order food at the local pizza shop. You tell the cashier the type of pizza you want. The cashier passes this information to the cook, who gathers ingredients and puts a pizza in the oven. The cook hands a finished pizza to the cashier, who collects payment and completes the workflow by handing over your pizza. The work *flows*, to the cashier, then to the cook, and then back again.

During each of these steps, all parties are also evaluating rules and making decisions. Before accepting the order, the cook has to compare the order against the ingredients in stock. The cashier has to validate and process any coupons you might present, and notify the manager if you pay with a counterfeit looking bill.

Not every workflow has to involve humans (which is good, because humans complicate even the simplest process). A workflow can take place between two distributed software applications. For example, two content management applications might need to follow a specific set of steps and rules when synchronizing content in the middle of the night.

Most workflows are stateful, and often run for a relatively long time. Hopefully, your pizza will be ready within 30 minutes. During those 30 minutes, state information about your order, like the toppings you selected, has to be available. A different workflow happens when the pizza shop orders cheese. The cheese supplier might not deliver the mozzarella for 30 hours, and the pizza shop may not pay the cheese supplier for 30 days. During those 30 days, something needs to maintain the state of the workflow for a purchase.

A workflow may spend a large portion of its lifetime waiting for events to happen in the world around it. A workflow may be idle when waiting for a delivery, or waiting for a payment, or waiting for a pizza to finish in the oven. During these wait times, the workflow is idle and no resources are required by the workflow.

A workflow, then, is a series of steps to finish a task. A workflow is often long running and stateful, and often needs to wait on events and interact with humans. You can see workflows everywhere you look in the world. As software developers, we often have to codify the workflows around us into software applications.

Building Workflow Solutions

We've all been involved with software projects that try to improve a business process. The process might have involved pizza orders, or financial transactions, or health care. Invariably, the word *workflow* will arise as we talk about these projects. While the workflow might sound simple, we know the devil is always in the details. We'll need database tables and data access classes to manage the workflow state. We'll need components to send emails and components to wait for messages to arrive in a queue. We will also need to express the workflow itself for the computer to execute. Let's look at a theoretical implementation of a workflow:

```
// The workflow for a newly submitted Purchase Order
class PurchaseOrderWorkflow
{
    public void Execute(PurchaseOrder order)
    {
        WaitForManagerApproval(order);
        NotifyPurchaseManager(order);
        WaitForGoods(order);
    }

    ...

}
```

Assuming we have definitions for the three methods inside of Execute, can a workflow really look this simple? The answer is no. We'll have to add code for exception handling, logging, and diagnostics. We'll need to raise events and provide hooks to track and cancel a running workflow. Also, this workflow will be idle and waiting for an external event to occur, like the arrival of the purchased goods, for the majority of the time. We can't expect to block a running application thread for days or weeks while waiting for a delivery. We'll need to provide a mechanism to save the workflow's state of execution to a persistent data store and remove the running workflow instance from memory. When a significant event occurs, we'll need to restore the workflow state and resume execution.

Unfortunately, we will have so much code in and around the workflow that we will lose sight of the workflow itself. All the supporting code will hide the process we are trying to model. A non-technical businessperson will never be able to look at the code and see the workflow. A developer will need to dig through the code to find the workflow inside.

An improved workflow design will try to separate the definition of a workflow from the engine and supporting code that executes the workflow. This type of approach allows a developer, or even a businessperson, to express *what* the workflow should be, while the workflow engine takes care of *how* to execute the workflow. These days, many workflow solutions define workflows inside the loving embrace of angled brackets. Let's look at some theoretical XML for a workflow definition:

```
<Workflow Name="PurchaseOrderWorkflow">
    <Steps>
        <WaitForTask Event="ManagerApproval"/>
        <NotifyTask Target="PurchaseManager"/>
        <WaitForTask Event="Delivery"/>
    </Steps>
    <Parameters>
        <Parameter Type="PurchaseOrder" Name="order"/>
    </Parameters>
</Workflow>
```

Let's ask the question again — can a workflow really look this simple? The answer is yes; what we will need is a workflow engine that understands this XML, and can transform the XML into instructions for the computer. The engine will include all the required features like exception handling, tracking, and enabling cancellations.

The C# code we saw earlier is an example of **imperative** programming. With imperative programming, we describe *how* to perform a task by providing a series of instructions to execute. The XML markup above is an example of **declarative** programming. With declarative programming, we describe *what* the task looks like, and let other software determine the steps required to complete the task. Most of the commercial workflow solutions on the market allow a declarative definition of workflow, because the declarative approach doesn't become cluttered with exception handling, event raising, and other lower-level details.

One of the benefits to using XML is the large number of tools with the ability to read, modify, create, and transform XML. XML is tool-able. Compared to parsing C# code, it would be relatively easy to parse the XML and generate a visualization of the workflow using blocks and arrows. Conversely, we could let a business user connect blocks together in a visual designer, and generate XML from a diagram.

Let's think about what we want in a workflow solution. We want to specify workflows in a declarative manner, perhaps with the aid of a visual designer. We want to feed workflow definitions into a workflow engine. The engine will manage errors, events, tracking, activation, and de-activation.

Enter Windows Workflow Foundation.

A Windows Workflow Tour

Microsoft's Windows Workflow Foundation is one piece of the new .NET 3.0 platform. The other major additions in .NET 3.0 include Windows Presentation Foundation, or WPF, and Windows Communication Foundation, or WCF. Microsoft will support Windows Workflow (WF) on Windows XP, Windows Server 2003, and Windows Vista.

Support for current and future Microsoft platforms means WF could reach near ubiquity over time. We can use WF in smart client applications, and in simple console-mode programs. We can also use WF in server-side applications, including Windows services, and ASP.NET web applications and web services. WF will make an appearance in several of Microsoft's own products, including Windows SharePoint Services and Microsoft Biztalk Server. We will now look at an overview of the essential features of Windows Workflow.

Activities

The primary building block in Windows Workflow is the **activity**. Activities compose the steps, or tasks in a workflow, and define the workflow. We can arrange activities into a hierarchy and feed activities to the workflow engine as instructions to execute. The activities can direct workflows involving both software and humans.

All activities in WF derive from an Activity base class. The Activity class defines operations common to all activities in a workflow, like Execute and Cancel. The class also defines common properties, like Name and Parent, as well as common events like Executing and Closed (the Closed event fires when an Activity is finished executing). The screenshot below shows the **Activity** class in the Visual Studio 2005 class designer:

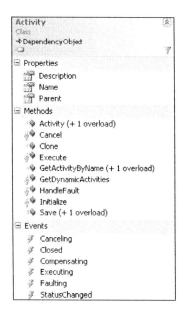

WF ships with a set of ready-made activities in the **base activity library**. The primitive activities in the library provide a foundation to build upon, and include control-flow operations, like the IfElseActivity and the WhileActivity. The base activity library also includes activities to wait for events, to invoke web services, to execute a rules engine, and more.

Custom Activities

Windows Workflow allows developers to extend the functionality of the base activity library by creating custom activities to solve problems in their specific domain. For instance, pizza delivery workflows could benefit from custom activities like SendOrderToKitchen or NotifyCustomer.

All custom activities will also ultimately derive from the base `Activity` class. The workflow engine makes no special distinction between activities written by Microsoft and custom activities written by third parties.

We can use custom activities to create domain-specific languages for building workflow solutions. A domain-specific language can greatly simplify a problem space. For instance, a `SendOrderToKitchen` custom activity could encapsulate a web service call and other processing logic inside. This activity is obviously specific to the restaurant problem domain. A developer will be more productive working with this higher-level abstraction than with the primitive activities in the base activity library. Even a restaurant manager will understand `SendOrderToKitchen` and might arrange the activity in a visual workflow designer. It will be difficult to find a restaurant manger who feels comfortable arranging `WhileActivity` and `InvokeWebServiceActivity` objects in a workflow designer.

C#, VB.NET, and XML are *general-purpose* languages and have the ability to solve a wide array of different problems. We can use C# to develop solutions for pizza restaurants as well as hospitals, and the language works equally well in either domain. A *domain-specific* language excels at solving problems in a particular area. A domain-specific language for restaurant workflow would boost productivity when writing software for a restaurant, but would not be as effective when writing software for a hospital.

Visual Studio 2005 Extensions

Microsoft also provides the Microsoft Visual Studio 2005 Extensions for Windows Workflow. These extensions plug into Visual Studio to provide a number of features, including a visual designer for constructing workflows. A screenshot of the visual designer is shown on the next page.

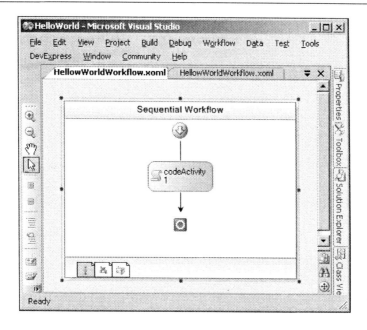

The designer uses the same windows we've come to love as Windows and web form developers. The **Toolbox** window will list the activities available to drag onto the design surface. We can add our own custom activities to the **Toolbox**. Once an activity is on the design surface, the **Properties** window will list the activity's properties that we can configure, and the events we can handle. The **Toolbox** window is shown below:

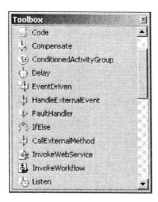

Windows Workflow and XAML

The WF designer can generate C# and Visual Basic code to represent our workflow. The designer can also read and write eXtensible Application Markup Language (XAML, pronounced zammel). XAML files are valid XML files. XAML brings a declarative programming model to Windows Workflow. Here is the XAML generated by the designer for the workflow we saw earlier:

```
<SequentialWorkflowActivity
    xmlns:x="http://schemas.microsoft.com/winfx/2006/xaml"
    xmlns="http://schemas.microsoft.com/winfx/2006/xaml/workflow"
    x:Class="HelloWorld.HellowWorldWorkflow"
    >

    <CodeActivity
        x:Name="codeActivity1"
        ExecuteCode="codeActivity1_ExecuteCode_1" />

</SequentialWorkflowActivity>
```

Our workflow is trivial and contains only a single activity inside—a `CodeActivity`. When the workflow engine executes the `CodeActivity`, the `CodeActivity` will invoke a method specified by the `ExecuteCode` attribute. Our XML also includes special XML namespace directives. We'll cover XAML and these namespaces in Chapter 2.

XAML is not a technology specific to Windows Workflow. As an "extensible application" markup language, XAML is also present in Microsoft's presentation framework—Windows Presentation Foundation (WPF). In WPF, XAML declaratively constructs a rich user interface consisting of not only buttons and labels, but also animation storyboards and data templates.

One important capability of declarative XAML is the ability to join forces with imperative code in a **partial** class. Partial classes, introduced in .NET 2.0, are a feature available to both Visual Basic and C# developers. Partial classes allow the definition of a class to span more than one file. The XAML above will transform into a partial class by the name of `HelloWorldWorkflow`. We control the name of the class from XAML with the `x:Name` attribute in the root node. We can add members to the generated class by defining a class with the same name and with the `partial` keyword.

```
public partial class HelloWorldWorkflow
                    : SequentialWorkflowActivity
{
    private void codeActivity1_ExecuteCode_1(object sender,
                                             EventArgs e)
    {
        // ...
    }
}
```

In this example, we are adding the `codeActivity1_ExecuteCode_1` method as a member of the same class (`HelloWorldWorkflow`) produced by the XAML.

WF Validation and Debugging

Another job of the workflow designer is to provide validation feedback for the activities in a workflow. Each activity can define its own design-time and run-time validation. The designer will flag an activity with a red exclamation point if the activity raises validation errors. For example, a `CodeActivity` will display a red exclamation point until we set the `ExecuteCode` property. Without a method to invoke, the `CodeActivity` is useless, but the validation catches this problem early and provides visual feedback.

The designer also provides debugging features. We can set breakpoints on an activity in the workflow designer. When execution stops, we can look at the **Call Stack** window to see the activities previously executed in the workflow instance. The debugger commands **Step In**, **Step Out**, and **Step Over** all work intuitively; for instance, the **Step In** command will move to the first activity inside a composite activity, while **Step Over** executes the entire composite activity and moves to the next sibling.

Designer Looks

The workflow designer allows customization of its design surface via **themes**. A theme defines the background colors, fonts, grid lines, and border styles to use on the design surface. We can even specify color and border styles for specific activity types. Through Visual Studio, we can create new themes, or modify existing themes.

All this styling ability isn't just to make the designer look pretty in Visual Studio, however. The WF designer is a component we can host inside our own applications. The ability to host the designer opens a number of interesting possibilities. First, we can host the designer and allow the non-developer types (a.k.a. business people) to design and edit workflows. By providing custom activities, we can match the vocabulary needed to build a workflow with a vocabulary the business people will understand (a domain-specific language). By providing custom themes, we can match the designer look with the look of our application.

The Windows Workflow Runtime

One perspective for Window Workflow is to view the workflow activities as instructions, or opcodes, for a workflow processor to execute. In Windows Workflow, the processor is in the WF runtime. To start a workflow party, we first need a host for the runtime and workflow services.

Hosting the Windows Workflow Runtime

Windows Workflow is not a stand-alone application. Like ASP.NET, WF lives inside a handful of assemblies (most notably for this topic, the `System.Workflow.Runtime.dll` assembly). Like the ASP.NET runtime, WF needs a host process to load, initialize, and start its runtime before anything interesting can happen. Unlike the traditional server-side usage of ASP.NET, however, WF will be useful in a variety of different hosts. We can host WF in a smart client application, a console application, or a Windows service, for instance.

The class diagram in the screenshot below features the primary classes we use to execute workflows in WF.

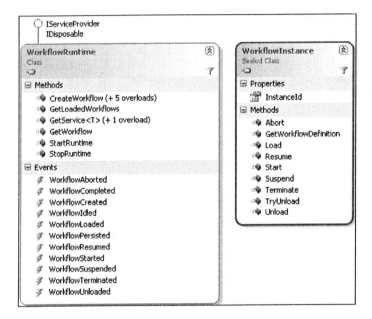

Creating an instance of the `WorkflowRuntime` class and calling `StartRuntime` is all we need to spin up the workflow execution environment. `WorkflowRuntime` defines methods that allow customization of the execution environment. The class also defines events we can listen for during execution. The runtime will fire an event when workflows finish execution, abort, turn idle, and more.

Once we've created an instance of the runtime, we can create workflows with the `CreateWorkflow` method. The `CreateWorkflow` method returns an object of type `WorkflowInstance`. The `WorkflowInstance` class represents an individual workflow. The `Start` method on the workflow instance object will begin the execution of a workflow. If an exception occurs, the workflow will invoke the `Terminate` method (which leads to the runtime raising a `WorkflowTerminated` event). A typical sequence of calls is shown in the screenshot next.

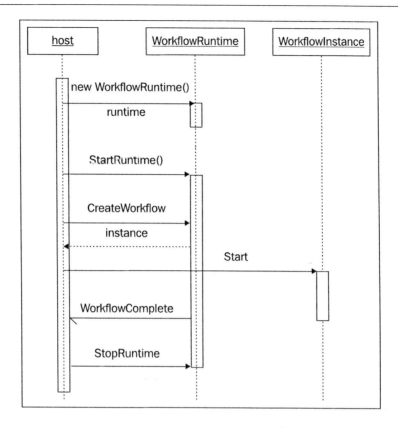

The WorkflowRuntime and WorkflowInstance classes are arguably the most important classes needed at run time, but they are not the only classes available. Other classes inside the WF assemblies provide important services to the workflow runtime. Chapter 5 will cover these services in detail, but the following provides a brief introduction.

Runtime Services

The WorkflowRuntime class provides only the basic features for executing workflows. Earlier, we mentioned important features we'd like to see in a workflow engine, like the ability to track active workflows and deactivate idle workflows. Don't worry, these features are available through an extensibility mechanism of WorkflowRuntime — the AddService method.

AddService allows us to make one or more **services** available to the runtime. These services might be custom services we've written specifically for our domain, like a custom scheduling service, or they might be services already written by Microsoft and included with WF. Let's continue our tour by looking at the services already available.

Scheduling Services

A scheduling service controls threads the runtime needs to execute workflows. The `DefaultWorkflowSchedulerService` creates new threads to execute workflows. Because the threads are separate from the host application, the workflows do not block any application threads and execute asynchronously. The maximum number of simultaneously executing workflows is configurable.

A second scheduling service, the `ManualWorkflowSchedulerService`, is available when the host application is willing to donate threads to the workflow runtime. Donating a thread to the runtime is a useful technique in server-side applications, like ASP.NET web applications and web services. Server-side applications typically pull a thread from a pool to service each client request. It makes sense to loan the thread to the WF runtime, and let the runtime execute the workflow synchronously on the existing request thread instead of using two threads per request, which could reduce scalability.

As with all services in Windows Workflow, you can define your own scheduling service if the built-in services do not fit your requirements.

Transaction Services

A transaction service, as the name might imply, allows the runtime to keep the internal state of a workflow consistent with the state in a durable store, like a relational database. The default transactional service is an instance of the `DefaultWorkflowTransactionService` class. Activities inside a running instance of a workflow, and the services operating on the same instance, can all share the same transaction context.

WF relies on the implementation of transactions in .NET's `System.Transactions` namespace. The `Transaction` class offers a lightweight, auto-enlisting, and promotable transaction. The transaction can start as a local transaction, and later the runtime can promote the transaction to a heavyweight, distributed transaction if needed.

Persistence Services

A persistence service is responsible for saving the state of a workflow to a durable store. The `SqlWorkflowPersistenceService` service saves the state of a workflow into a SQL Server database. Persistence is required for long-running workflows, because we can't have an invoice-processing workflow in memory for 30 days till the customer's payment arrives. Instead, the runtime can persist the state of the workflow to a durable store and unload the instance from memory. In 30 days (or hopefully, less), the runtime can reload the workflow instance and resume processing. The WF runtime will automatically persist a workflow that is idle or suspended when a persistence service is present.

The `SqlWorkflowPersistenceService` will work with SQL Server 2000 or any later version of Microsoft SQL Server, including the free MSDE and Express editions. Of course, we'll need a database schema that the persistence service understands. In Chapter 5 we will see how to use the T-SQL installation scripts provided by the .NET 3.0 installation.

Tracking Services

While a scheduling service is responsible for selecting threads for a workflow to run on, a tracking service is responsible for monitoring and recording information about the execution of a workflow. A tracking service will tell the runtime the type of information it wants to know about workflows using a **tracking profile**. Once the service establishes a profile, the service can open a **tracking channel** to receive events and data. Chapter 5 includes more details on tracking profiles and channels.

WF includes a `SqlTrackingService` class that stores tracking data into a SQL Server database. The service will use the previously discussed transactional service to ensure the tracking data for a workflow is consistent with the state of the workflow it's tracking. The runtime does not start a tracking service by default, but we can programmatically add a tracking service (or configure a tracking service with an application configuration file) for the runtime to use.

Now we've covered all the basic features of WF, so let's put the software to work.

Our First Workflow

Maybe you've had one of those product managers who is always at your desk, asking "are you done, yet?" In this section, we will replace the annoying project manager with a trivial Windows Workflow program. The sample isn't meant to demonstrate all the capabilities of the platform, but give a general feel for creating and running a workflow with WF.

Before we can begin, we'll need to download and install the .NET 3.0 framework. The installation program is available from `http://netfx3.com`. Supported development tools for the .NET 3.0 framework include all editions of Visual Studio 2005. We'll also need to download and install Visual Studio 2005 Extensions for Windows Workflow Foundation. The extensions are also available from `http://netfx3.com`. The extensions are not compatible with the Express editions of Visual Studio 2005.

First, we'll use Visual Studio to create a new Workflow project (**File | New Project**). We'll choose C# as our language and select the **Sequential Workflow Console Application** template (see the screenshot on the next page). The template gives us a project with references to all the correct WF assemblies, an empty workflow, and a `Program.cs` file to drive the workflow. Right-click the workflow and select **Delete** so we can start a workflow from scratch.

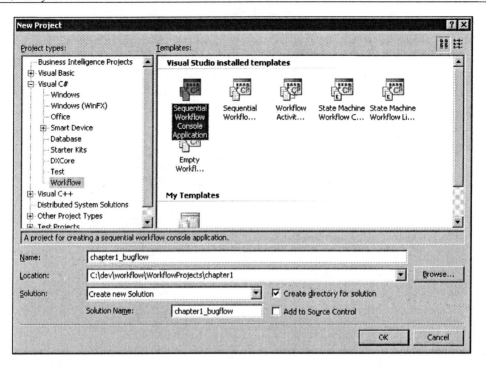

We can now right-click the project file in the **Solution Explorer** window and select **Add New Item**. From the list of items we'll choose **Sequential Workflow (with code separation)** and give the item the name of **workflow1.xoml** (see screenshot below). This XOML file will contain the XAML definition of our workflow.

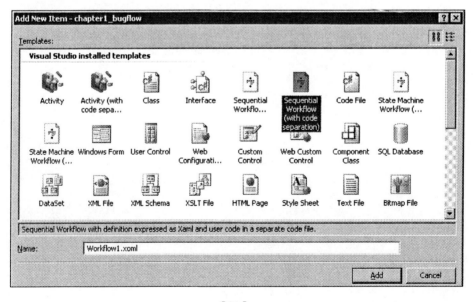

If we click to expand the node containing **Workflow1.xoml**, we will find a C# code-beside file (`Workflow1.xoml.cs`) containing a partial class. As we mentioned earlier, the partial class will combine with the class generated from the XAML to produce a single type. Let's modify the class in `Workflow1.xoml.cs` by adding an `IsFixed` property with a backing field, as shown below:

```
public partial class Workflow1 : SequentialWorkflowActivity
{
    private bool _isFixed;
    public bool IsFixed
    {
        get { return _isFixed; }
        set { _isFixed = value; }
    }
}
```

If we double-click the `.xoml` file, the designer will appear. At this point we would want to open the **Toolbox** window if is not open (*Ctrl+Alt+X*). We can drag a **While** activity from the **Toolbox** and drop the activity between the start and end point of our workflow. The **While** Activity executes a child task until some condition is met. Our next step is to drag a **Code** activity from the **Toolbox** into the center of the **While** activity. At this point, our designer should resemble the following screenshot:

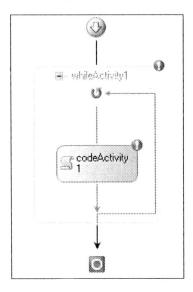

Notice both activities display a red exclamation point. The activities are failing their validation checks. We can hover the mouse cursor over the exclamation points and open a smart tag to view the validation error. If we tried to compile the program we'd see these same validation errors as compilation errors. We'll fix these errors now.

The **Code** activity requires us to assign an event handler for the `ExecuteCode` event. We can set the event by opening the **Properties** window (*F4*) and clicking the **Code activity** to set focus. Double-clicking in the empty space beside the **ExecuteCode** property will send us into the code-beside file and generate a new event handler. We can place the following code into the event handler. This code will ask the user if a bug is fixed, and then read a key press. If the user presses the 'y' key, the code will set the `_isFixed` field to `true`.

```
private void codeActivity1_ExecuteCode(object sender, EventArgs e)
{
    Console.WriteLine("Is the bug fixed?");

    Char answer = Console.ReadKey().KeyChar;
    answer = Char.ToLower(answer);

    if (answer == 'y')
    {
        _isFixed = true;
    }
    else
    {
        Console.WriteLine();
        Console.WriteLine("Get back to work!");
        Console.WriteLine();
    }
}
```

The **Code activity** should now pass validation, so we can turn our attention to the **While activity**. A **While activity** requires a valid `Condition` property. Several activities in the base activity library work with conditions, including the `IfElse`, `ConditionedActivityGroup`, and `Replicator` activities. Chapter 9 will cover conditions and rules in more detail.

We can set the **Condition** property of our activity by opening the drop-down list beside the **Condition** property in the **Properties** window. We have the choice of selecting a **CodeCondition** or a **RuleConditionReference**. These choices represent the two techniques available to express a condition, the first being with code (a method that returns a Boolean value), the second being with a rule. Let's select the **RuleConditionReference**. A rule condition is a named expression that evaluates to true or false, and can live in an external `.rules` file for easy maintenance. A plus sign appears beside the **Condition** property, and we can click the sign to expand the property editor.

When the **Condition** property expands, the **Property** window gives us the ability to set a **ConditionName** and an **Expression**. Clicking on the ellipsis (**...**) button in the **Condition** name will launch a **Select Condition** dialog box.

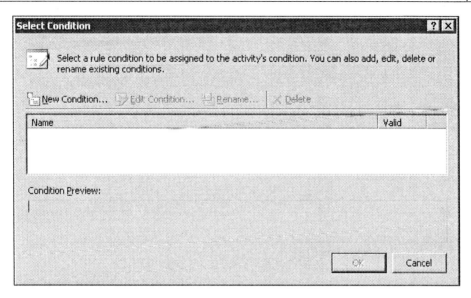

Clicking the **New Condition...** button will launch the **Rule Condition Editor**.

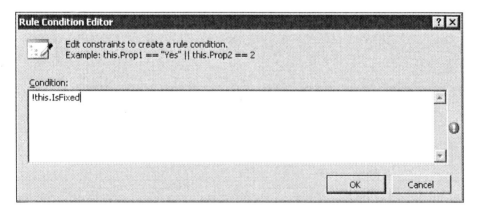

We want the **While activity** to loop until the bug is fixed. Our rule is `!this.IsFixed`. Once we've entered the condition (notice the editor provides IntelliSense), we can click **OK**. When we return to the **Select Condition** dialog box, we can see the editor has given our condition the name of **Condition1**. We should select **Condition1** and press **OK**. The **While activity** should now have a **ConditionName** and **Expression** set, and pass validation.

Now we need to open the `Program.cs` file, which contains the method `Main`—the entry point for our Console application. We need to host the WF runtime and ask the runtime to execute our workflow. The item template for a workflow project provides all the boilerplate code we need. Let's review the code:

```
class Program
{
    static void Main(string[] args)
    {
        WorkflowRuntime workflowRuntime = new WorkflowRuntime();

        workflowRuntime.WorkflowCompleted +=
            new EventHandler<WorkflowCompletedEventArgs>
                (workflowRuntime_WorkflowCompleted);

        workflowRuntime.WorkflowTerminated +=
            new EventHandler<WorkflowTerminatedEventArgs>
                (workflowRuntime_WorkflowTerminated);

        WorkflowInstance instance;
        instance = workflowRuntime.CreateWorkflow(typeof(Workflow1));
        instance.Start();

        waitHandle.WaitOne();
    }

    static void workflowRuntime_WorkflowTerminated(object sender,
                                    WorkflowTerminatedEventArgs e)
    {
        Console.WriteLine(e.Exception.Message);
        waitHandle.Set();
    }

    static void workflowRuntime_WorkflowCompleted(object sender,
                                    WorkflowCompletedEventArgs e)
    {
        waitHandle.Set();
    }

    static AutoResetEvent waitHandle = new AutoResetEvent(false);
}
```

The first step is to instantiate a WorkflowRuntime instance. The code wires up
event handlers to the runtime so we know if a workflow terminates (because of
an exception), or completes successfully. The code instantiates our bug-fixing
workflow using the CreateWorkflow method, passing the type of our workflow.
Since the workflow engine executes our workflow asynchronously, we need to block
our thread on an AutoResetEvent object and wait for the workflow to complete
(otherwise, the console mode program would exit before the workflow gets an
opportunity to run). An AutoResetEvent object will block a thread until the object is
in a signaled state, which we do with the Set event in the event handlers.

We can now build our workflow solution and run the executable from the command line.

```
Command Prompt

C:\dev\workflow\WorkflowProjects\chapter1_bugflow\bin\Debug>
chapter1_bugflow.exe
Is the bug fixed?
n
Get back to work!

Is the bug fixed?
n
Get back to work!

Is the bug fixed?
n
Get back to work!

Is the bug fixed?
y
C:\dev\workflow\WorkflowProjects\chapter1_bugflow\bin\Debug>
```

Summary

Software developers have been implementing workflows to model business processes since the beginning of time. During this time, we've learned that workflows can be long-running and often require input from humans. Building a robust workflow to meet these challenges is a daunting task. An ideal paradigm for building workflows is to separate the workflow definition from the engine that executes the workflow.

Once we've separated workflow definitions from the execution engine, we can go on to build workflow components to create a domain-specific language. A businessperson has the ability to understand the domain-specific language, and can understand a workflow without seeing the clutter of exception handling and workflow tracking.

Windows Workflow brings a workflow engine and workflow development tools to Microsoft platforms. The instructions for the WF engine are activities, and we can arrange these activities using a graphical designer, XAML, code, or a combination of the three. WF provides the services we need for a workflow engine, including persistence, threading, and transaction services. The future looks bright for building workflow solutions.

2
Authoring Workflows

The workflow designer hosted in Visual Studio 2005 makes workflow design a drag-and-drop operation. In this chapter, we will build a workflow with the designer, and then take a detailed look at what happens behind the scenes. Ultimately, the workflow definition we see in the designer becomes a type in a .NET assembly. Because Windows Workflow is flexible, there are several paths available for the workflow to journey from designer to compiled type.

One approach is to author our workflows using a purely declarative style (using only XAML). We can also author workflows using a purely imperative style (using only C# or Visual Basic code). Finally, we can use a combination of XAML and code.

When a workflow is executing, these different approaches won't have a noticeable impact. When we are building workflows, however, the authoring styles offer various strengths and weaknesses we can align with our needs. We will examine the pros and cons of the available approaches and see how a workflow moves from design to executable instructions.

Pure Code

Building a workflow with a pure code approach means we are only using C# or Visual Basic code to define the workflow. There is no XAML involved. This doesn't mean *we* have to write all the code ourselves. Many designers in Visual Studio, like the Windows forms designer, have been generating C# and Visual Basic code for years. The workflow designer has the ability to generate code for us. We will want to combine the designer-generated code with our own code to build a workflow.

Pure Code and Visual Studio

The Visual Studio 2005 Extensions for Windows Workflow package will add project and item templates into Visual Studio. These item templates provide a starting point for building a workflow project, a workflow, or an activity.

To use an item template we merely need to right-click a project and select **Add | New Item**. One of the item templates appearing in the **Add New Item** dialog box sets up the files and code needed to support a **pure code** approach. This item template is the **Sequential Workflow (code)** template. Other item templates appear in the screenshot below:

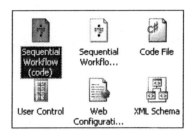

When we add a workflow to our project using the **Sequential Workflow (code)** template, we don't add just a single source code file. If we create a new workflow from the template, and give the workflow the name of PureCode, the template will add two files to the project: a PureCode.cs file and a PureCode.Designer.cs file. PureCode.cs is a file we can edit. The PureCode.Designer.cs file contains code the graphical designer will edit.

With our PureCode workflow in the designer window, we can drop a CodeActivity from the **Toolbox** window into the designer. We can then use the **Properties** window to assign a method for the ExecuteCode event. Select the CodeActivity, and then click the **Generate Handlers** hyperlink in the **Properties** window to generate a default handler for ExecuteCode.

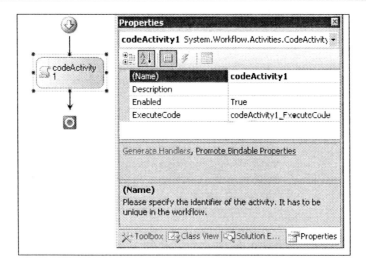

All the steps listed above will produce the following code inside of `PureCode.cs`.

```csharp
using System;
using System.Workflow.Activities;

namespace chapter2_library
{
  public sealed partial class PureCode: SequentialWorkflowActivity
  {
    public PureCode()
    {
      InitializeComponent();
    }
    private void codeActivity1_ExecuteCode(object sender,
                                              EventArgs e)
    {
    }
  }
}
```

PureCode.cs is our file to edit. The `codeActivity1_ExecuteCode` method is here and waiting for us to provide an implementation. Notice the constructor calls a method by the name of `InitializeComponent`, but this method is not present in the `PureCode.cs` file. As it turns out, the `InitializeComponent` method *is* a member of the `PureCode` class, but we will find its definition in another file. This is the magic provided by the `partial` keyword modifier on our class. The `partial` keyword allows us to split a class definition across multiple source code files.

The rest of the class definition for our `PureCode` workflow lives in
PureCode.Designer.cs. We typically would never need to look at or edit this
class, because the workflow designer is responsible for generating code inside
the file. Here is what the designer generates for this workflow.

```
using System;
using System.Workflow.Activities;

namespace chapter2_library
{
  public sealed partial class PureCode
  {
    #region Designer generated code

    private void InitializeComponent()
    {
        this.CanModifyActivities = true;
        this.codeActivity1 = new
            System.Workflow.Activities.CodeActivity();
        //
        // codeActivity1
        //
        this.codeActivity1.Name = "codeActivity1";
        this.codeActivity1.ExecuteCode +=
            new System.EventHandler(
                this.codeActivity1_ExecuteCode);
        //
        // PureCode
        //
        this.Activities.Add(this.codeActivity1);
        this.Name = "PureCode";
        this.CanModifyActivities = false;

    }

    #endregion

    private CodeActivity codeActivity1;

  }
}
```

The `InitializeComponent` method appears in this half of the partial class definition
and contains the code to set up the activities in our workflow. In this case, we have
only a single `Code` activity in our workflow. The code constructs the activity and
adds the activity as a child of the workflow. The class also defines private fields for
each activity in our workflow — in this case only `codeActivity1`. We can control
the names of the activity fields by setting the `Name` property of an activity in the
Property window.

When we build our project, the C# compiler will merge the two partial class definitions into a single type. The new type will have the name of PureCode and contain both the InitializeComponent and codeActivity1_ExecuteCode methods as shown in the figure below:

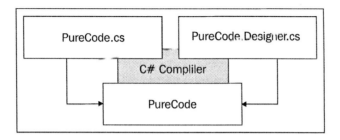

With the pure code approach of Visual Studio, each workflow is the combination of a designer-managed code file, and a developer-managed code file. This is a perfectly reasonable approach if we construct all of our workflows using the designer. Of course, it would also be possible to write all that code by hand, or with a different tool. The ultimate goal is to create a hierarchical tree of activities inside our workflow. Some of the alternative approaches to defining workflows are more amiable to outside tools.

Objects and Their Relationships

A workflow ultimately becomes a group of managed objects in memory. The trick is to arrange the objects in a relationship so they can perform useful work. This trick isn't specific to workflow software. Consider some code from a Windows application:

```
button1 = new System.Windows.Forms.Button();
button1.Location = new System.Drawing.Point(13, 13);
button1.Name = "button1";
button1.Size = new System.Drawing.Size(75, 23);
button1.Text = "Click Me!";
this.Controls.Add(this.button1);
```

This code is similar to the code we saw in the InitializeComponent method the workflow designer created earlier. Instead of arranging activities, this code is arranging user interface controls. The code creates a Button object and sets some properties so the button will appear visually appealing. This code lives inside a class derived from System.Windows.Forms.Form. The most important line of code is adding the button object to the form's Controls collection: this.Controls. Add(this.button1). If we never established a relationship between the Form object and the Button object, the button would never appear on the form.

We generally don't write code like this ourselves, but we rely on a designer to generate the code. The designer-generated code has two goals. The first goal is to instantiate objects and set their properties to an initial value. The second goal is to establish relationships between the new objects and construct the relationships between the objects.

The ASP.NET designer-generated code for a web form has the same goals, but looks a bit different:

```
<asp:Panel runat="server" ID="panel1">
    <asp:Button runat="server" ID="button1" Text="Click Me!" />
</asp:Panel>
```

The ASP.NET designer produces declarative mark-up instead of imperative code. Arguably, the primary reason for using declarative mark-up is the ability to intertwine .NET objects with HTML, and HTML is already a declarative language. However, using a declarative style increases readability of the generated code. At a glance, we can see the Button object is a child of the Panel object.

Both Windows Presentation Foundation and Windows Workflow use the eXtensible Application Markup Language (XAML), which takes the declarative style even further.

```
<Grid>
    <Button Grid.Row="0" Grid.Column="0">
            Click Me!
    </Button>
</Grid>
```

XAML has the advantage of being valid XML. We are now looking at a declarative style that is human readable (it's easy to see the Button as a child of the Grid control), and tool-able. Tool-able meaning we don't have to rely on custom designers and compilers to read, write, modify, and parse the mark-up. We could write a custom tool for special tasks using the wide variety of XML technologies available, like XPath, XQuery, XSLT, and the XML DOM.

In the next section, we will look at using a purely declarative approach to building workflows using XAML.

Pure XAML

Here is the start of a workflow defined using only XAML.

```
<SequentialWorkflowActivity
  xmlns="http://schemas.microsoft.com/winfx/2006/xaml/workflow"
  xmlns:x="http://schemas.microsoft.com/winfx/2006/xaml"
```

```
x:Class="MyWorkflow"
>

<WhileActivity>
  <CodeActivity />
</WhileActivity>

</SequentialWorkflowActivity>
```

The root element is a SequentialWorkflowActivity. WF provides the SequentialWorkflowActivity and StateMachineWorkflowActivity classes primarily to serve as root level activities. These classes manage the execution of their children using different styles. The SequentialWorkflowActivity serially executes its children until the last activity completes. The order of activities inside a sequential workflow is important, as the order will determine when the activity executes. We'll look at the StateMachineWorkflowActivity in detail when we reach Chapter 7.

 The file extension for a XAML file containing workflow markup is .xoml.

Our workflow consists of a WhileActivity with a CodeActivity inside. The XAML is an XML representation of the tree of objects we want to create. The XAML sets up a CodeActivity to execute inside of a loop. We've yet to define the code, or the while condition, so the workflow will not pass validation as yet.

We talk about an XML element like <WhileActivity> as if the element was a class, because it is. XAML works by mapping XML to .NET types. Elements map to classes, and attributes map to properties on those classes. Each XML namespace in XAML corresponds to one or more .NET namespaces.

Namespaces in XML are similar to namespaces in .NET. Both help to avoid name collisions when different entities have the same name. Our XAML file brings two namespaces into scope with the xmlns attribute. The workflow namespace is the first and default namespace in our XAML, and maps to the CLR namespace System. Workflow.Activities. The workflow namespace is the default namespace because there is no prefix for the namespace. The second namespace is the XAML namespace, which uses an x: prefix.

The XAML namespace is special because it gives instructions to the workflow compiler. For instance, the x: Class attribute tells the workflow compiler the name of a new Type to create from the workflow definition. When we run the XAML through the compiler, the result will be an assembly with a class inside by the name of MyWorkflow.

For now, let's remove the WhileActivity and concentrate on putting together valid XAML to compile.

```
<SequentialWorkflowActivity
  xmlns="http://schemas.microsoft.com/winfx/2006/xaml/workflow"
  xmlns:x="http://schemas.microsoft.com/winfx/2006/xaml"
  x:Class="MyWorkflow"
  >

  <CodeActivity ExecuteCode="SayHello" />

  <x:Code>
    <![CDATA[
    private void SayHello(object sender, EventArgs e)
    {
      Console.WriteLine("Hello, workflow!");
    }
    ]]>
  </x:Code>

</SequentialWorkflowActivity>
```

We now have a valid workflow because the CodeActivity has an event handler defined for the ExecuteCode event. Our use of the CodeActivity is atypical. A CodeActivity would usually inspect and change the workflow state using some calculations and logic. We are just writing a message to the console. This example demonstrates how to use in-line code with XAML. The use of in-line code is also atypical, as many developers like to work with proper classes and consider in-line code one of the seven deadly sins.

If we really need to write to the console from inside a workflow, we might package the behavior into a custom activity. A custom activity encapsulates behavior and state into a component for easy reuse.

Using Custom Activities in XAML

A custom activity inherits from `System.Workflow.ComponentModel.Activity` and allows us to build workflows using components tailored to our problem domain. To implement a custom activity we need to override the virtual `Execute` method. The following code is a custom activity that can write a message to the console.

```csharp
using System;
using System.Workflow.ComponentModel;

namespace OdeToCode.WinWF.Activities
{
    public class WriteLineActivity : Activity
    {
        protected override ActivityExecutionStatus Execute
                (ActivityExecutionContext executionContext)
        {
            Console.WriteLine(_message);
            return ActivityExecutionStatus.Closed;
        }

        private string _message;
        public string Message
        {
            get { return _message; }
            set { _message = value; }
        }
    }
}
```

We've also created a public `Message` property for our custom activity. We can set a value for this property in XAML using a `Message` attribute. If we use this custom activity from our XAML file, we won't need to use in-line code. Our XAML now looks like the following:

```xml
<SequentialWorkflowActivity
    xmlns="http://schemas.microsoft.com/winfx/2006/xaml/workflow"
    xmlns:x="http://schemas.microsoft.com/winfx/2006/xaml"
    xmlns:otc="http://schemas.OdeToCode.com/WinWF/Activities"
    x:Class="MyWorkflow"
    >

    <otc:WriteLineActivity Message="Hello, workflow!"/>

</SequentialWorkflowActivity>
```

Notice we've defined a new XML namespace where our custom activity lives. This is the `http://schemas.OdeToCode.com/WinWF/Activities` namespace. How will the workflow compiler use this namespace to look for the `WriteLineActivity` component? The answer is in a piece of assembly-level metadata we include in the assembly where the `WriteLineActivity` lives. This metadata provides a map between the XML namespace and the .NET namespace where our custom activity lives.

```
[assembly: XmlnsDefinition(
    "http://schemas.OdeToCode.com/WinWF/Activities",
    "OdeToCode.WinWF.Activities")
]
```

The XAML compiler will look in referenced assemblies for `XmlnsDefinitionAttribute` attributes. When it finds the above definition, the compiler will know to map `http://schemas.OdeToCode.com/WinWF/Activities` to the CLR namespace `OdeToCode.WinWF.Activities` in the assembly where the attribute resides.

An alternative approach to namespace mapping is to embed the CLR namespace and assembly name directly in the XAML. Assuming our custom activity is inside an assembly by the name of `Foo.dll`, this approach would look like the following: `xmlns:otc="clr-namespace:OdeToCode.WinWF.Activities;assembly=Foo"`. This alternative approach is useful when we need to use a type inside an assembly that we do not own, and we can't add metadata to the assembly. In all other cases, it is better to have the layer of indirection provided by an XML namespace as in our earlier example.

Our workflow is almost ready to execute, but first we will need to transform the XAML into instructions for the CLR.

Compiling Workflows

Windows Workflow provides two compilers for us to use. The first compiler is the class `WorkflowCompiler` in the `System.Workflow.ComponentModel.Compiler` namespace. The second compiler is a command-line compiler, essentially a console-mode application wrapper around the `WorkflowCompiler` class.

The workflow compiler follows a number of steps when it transforms a workflow definition into a `Type`. The first step is to validate every activity in the workflow definition. An activity can define its own validation logic. For example, the

`CodeActivity` will raise a validation error if its `ExecuteCode` event handler is empty. After validation, the compiler will generate code (the default language is C#) into a temporary directory. The generated source code then serves as input to the C# or Visual Basic.NET compiler for compilation into an assembly.

Compiling with Wfc.exe

The WF command-line compiler goes by the name of `wfc.exe` — the Windows Workflow Compiler. The first parameter we will pass is the name of our XOML file. Let's say we've placed our XAML into a file with the name of `purexaml3.xoml`. We will also pass the name of the assembly we want the compiler to produce (`purexaml3.dll`) using the `-out` parameter. If we have any custom activities defined in additional assemblies, we will need to reference those assemblies using a `-r` parameter. The following screenshot shows us referencing an executable assembly by the name of `chapter2_Host.exe`:

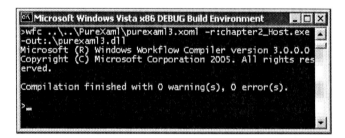

Voilà! We now have an assembly we can use in a host application. We can dynamically load the assembly using a call to `Type.GetType` and passing an **assembly-qualified** type name. An assembly-qualified type name includes the name of the `Type` and the name of the assembly where the `Type` lives. The `Type` name for our new workflow is `MyWorkflow`. This is the name we assigned using the `x:` `Class` attribute in the XOML file. The assembly-qualified name will be `MyWorkflow,` `purexaml3`. The following code instantiates and executes the workflow:

```
using (WorkflowRuntime runtime = new WorkflowRuntime())
using (AutoResetEvent waitHandle = new AutoResetEvent(false))
{
   runtime.WorkflowCompleted += delegate { waitHandle.Set(); };
   runtime.WorkflowTerminated += delegate { waitHandle.Set(); };

   Type workflowType = Type.GetType("MyWorkflow, purexaml3");
   WorkflowInstance instance = runtime.CreateWorkflow(workflowType);
   instance.Start();

   waitHandle.WaitOne();
}
```

Remember the workflow executes asynchronously on a thread from the Common Language Runtime (CLR) thread pool. We will wait for the workflow to finish by waiting for a signal from an `AutoResetEvent` event.

The CLR thread pool manages a group of background threads for asynchronous operations. Creating a thread is a relatively expensive operation, but the thread pool can amortize this cost over the lifetime of an application by re-using threads across multiple background operations. The runtime removes a thread from the pool when an operation is queued to work on a background thread. When the operation is complete, the runtime returns the thread to the pool to assign out again in the future.

Compiling with WorkflowCompiler

We can use the `WorkflowCompiler` and `WorkflowCompilerResults` classes to programmatically compile workflow definitions and retrieve a new assembly. The `Wfc.exe` uses the `WorkflowCompiler` class internally to perform a compilation. These classes are shown in the class diagram below:

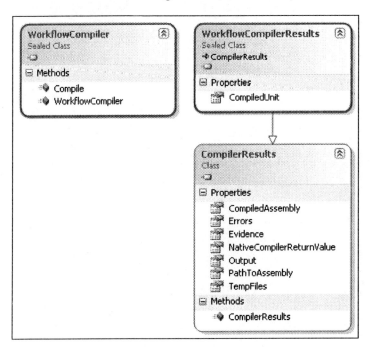

To use the `WorkflowCompiler` class, we need to set up a `WorkflowCompilerParameters` object. We can use the parameters object to reference any assemblies containing custom activities.

```
WorkflowCompiler compiler = new WorkflowCompiler();

WorkflowCompilerParameters parameters;
parameters = new WorkflowCompilerParameters();
parameters.GenerateInMemory = true;
parameters.ReferencedAssemblies.Add("chapter2_Host.exe");

string[] xomlFiles = { @"..\..\purexaml\purexaml3.xoml" };

WorkflowCompilerResults compilerResults;
compilerResults = compiler.Compile(parameters, xomlFiles);
```

Notice the `Compile` method accepts an array of string objects, so we can pass multiple XOML files at once. If the compilation was not successful, the `Errors` property of the result will contain details on what went wrong.

```
if (compilerResults.Errors.Count > 0)
{
  foreach (CompilerError error in compilerResults.Errors)
  {
    Console.WriteLine(error.ErrorText);
  }
}
```

Running the workflow compiled by the `WorkflowCompiler` only requires a slight adjustment to our previous code. Instead of using `Type.GetType` we will go directly to the new assembly and ask for the workflow type.

```
using (WorkflowRuntime runtime = new WorkflowRuntime())
using (AutoResetEvent waitHandle = new AutoResetEvent(false))
{
  runtime.WorkflowCompleted += delegate { waitHandle.Set(); };
  runtime.WorkflowTerminated += delegate { waitHandle.Set(); };

  Type workflowType;
  workflowType =
          compilerResults.CompiledAssembly.GetType("MyWorkflow");
  WorkflowInstance instance = runtime.CreateWorkflow(workflowType);

  instance.Start();

  waitHandle.WaitOne();
}
```

Two interesting implementation details are worth mentioning:

- First, the `WorkflowCompiler` creates a new application domain on each call to the `Compile` method. Be wary of the overhead when designing applications that may invoke the `Compile` method multiple times during their lifetime.

- Second, the `Compile` method will automatically load the new assembly into the current AppDomain if the `GenerateInMemory` parameter flag is set to true and the compilation is successful. If you don't want the assembly loaded immediately, make sure to set `GenerateInMemory` to false.

We'll be looking at workflow activation later, which is a lightweight alternative to compilation. For now, we have one more compilation environment to examine.

Compilation with MSBuild

MSBuild is the XML-based build engine included with the .NET 2.0 runtime. All of the `.csproj` and `.vbproj` project files used by Visual Studio are also MSBuild files. Whenever a developer asks Visual Studio 2005 to build a project, the IDE uses a hosted instance of MSBuild to perform the build. A developer could also use MSBuild directly from the command line and pass command-line options. The Windows Workflow install will register `.xoml` file extensions to build with MSBuild.

We are going to build our custom activity and workflow into the same assembly using MSBuild. We can use the same XOML file as the last example, and create an MSBuild project file.

```
<Project
    DefaultTargets="Build"
    xmlns="http://schemas.microsoft.com/developer/msbuild/2003">
  <PropertyGroup>
    <OutputType>library</OutputType>
    <AssemblyName>purexaml3</AssemblyName>
  </PropertyGroup>
  <ItemGroup>
    <Reference Include="System" />
    <Reference Include="System.Workflow.Activities" />
    <Reference Include="System.Workflow.ComponentModel" />
    <Reference Include="System.Workflow.Runtime" />
  </ItemGroup>
  <ItemGroup>
    <Compile Include="..\CustomActivity\WriteLineActivity.cs"/>
  </ItemGroup>
  <ItemGroup>
```

```
    <Content Include="purexaml3.xoml"/>
  </ItemGroup>
  <Import
    Project="$(MSBuildBinPath)\Microsoft.CSharp.targets" />
  <Import
    Project="$(MSBuildExtensionsPath)\Microsoft\Windows Workflow
  Foundation\v3.0\Workflow.Targets" />
</Project>
```

Our MSBuild file consists of properties, items, and targets. *Properties* configure the build by setting the output type and assembly name. *Items* represent the inputs to the build engine, like source code files and assembly references. We've included our XOML file as well as the C# source code file for the `WriteLineActivity`. Finally, we import targets for C# and workflow compilation. These targets will execute the necessary tasks to compile the code and workflow. When we create a new workflow project in Visual Studio, the project template automatically sets up the project file to import the workflow targets and reference the workflow assemblies.

To see the XML behind a project file, right-click a project file in Visual Studio and select **Unload Project** from the context menu. Right-click the project again and select the **Edit** option. The typical workflow project will contain more XML than the bare minimum we've defined above, but you'll notice all projects created by the workflow templates will have references to the workflow assemblies, and an import of the workflow target definitions.

At this point, all we need to do is execute MSBuild and pass the name of our new project file.

```
Microsoft Windows Vista x86 DEBUG Build Environment          _ □ ×

>msbuild purexaml3.csproj
Microsoft (R) Build Engine Version 2.0.50727.42
[Microsoft .NET Framework, Version 2.0.50727.42]
Copyright (C) Microsoft Corporation 2005. All rights reserved.

Build started 3/21/2006 4:24:20 PM.
_____
Project "C:\dev\workflow\WorkflowProjects\Chapter2\chapter2_Host\PureX
aml\purexaml3.csproj" (default targets):

Target XomlCompilation:
    Generated temporary code file: C:\Documents and Settings\bitmask\L
ocal Settings\Temp\mjjmxopr.cs
    XAML validations completed with 0 errors and 0 warnings.
Target CoreCompile:
    C:\WINDOWS\Microsoft.NET\Framework\v2.0.50727\Csc.exe /noconfig /n
owarn:1701,1702 /reference:C:\WINDOWS\Microsoft.NET\Framework\v2.0.507
27\System.dll /reference:"C:\Program Files\Reference Assemblies\Micros
oft\WinFx\v3.0\System.Workflow.Activities.dll" /reference:"C:\Program
Files\Reference Assemblies\Microsoft\WinFx\v3.0\System.Workflow.Compon
entModel.dll" /reference:"C:\Program Files\Reference Assemblies\Micros
oft\WinFx\v3.0\System.Workflow.Runtime.dll" /debug+ /out:obj\Debug\pur
examl3.dll /target:library ..\CustomActivity\WriteLineActivity.cs "C:\
Documents and Settings\bitmask\Local Settings\Temp\mjjmxopr.cs"
Target CopyFilesToOutputDirectory:
    Copying file from "obj\Debug\purexaml3.dll" to "bin\Debug\purexaml
3.dll".
    purexaml3 -> C:\dev\workflow\WorkflowProjects\Chapter2\chapter2_Ho
st\PureXaml\bin\Debug\purexaml3.dll
    Copying file from "obj\Debug\purexaml3.pdb" to "bin\Debug\purexaml
3.pdb".
Target XomlCompilationCleanup:
    Deleting file "C:\Documents and Settings\bitmask\Local Settings\Te
mp\mjjmxopr.cs".

Build succeeded.
    0 Warning(s)
    0 Error(s)

Time Elapsed 00:00:02.21

>_
```

Notice the XOML compilation phase generates C# code into a temporary directory, similar to how ASP.NET compiles web forms. MSBuild feeds the temporary source code and the project source code to the C# compiler. This is an important step to remember, because our code will compile at the same time as the temporary code created from the workflow markup. We will see later how this approach will let us extend the workflow type with our code.

Note that in a Visual Basic project, the code generated from the XOML compilation is Visual Basic code. Visual Basic workflow projects import a different targets file: `Workflow.VisualBasic.Targets`.

Code Generation and XAML Serialization

We mentioned earlier that the workflow compiler generates source code from XAML as part of the compilation process. When using MSBuild, the destination for the source code is a temporary directory, but we can ask the command-line compiler to generate a permanent file using the parameter /t:codegen. Let's ask the workflow compiler to generate code from a XOML file instead of creating an assembly. C# is the default language the compiler will use. Visual Basic is also available as an option (/language:vb).

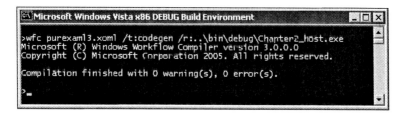

The generated source code looks like the source code below (except that some extraneous namespaces and compiler directives were removed):

```csharp
using OdeToCode.WinWF.Activities;
using System.Workflow.Activities;

public partial class MyWorkflow : SequentialWorkflowActivity
{
    private WriteLineActivity writeLineActivity1;

    public MyWorkflow()
    {
        this.InitializeComponent();
    }

    private void InitializeComponent()
    {
        this.CanModifyActivities = true;

        this.writeLineActivity1 = new WriteLineActivity();
        this.writeLineActivity1.Message = "Hello, workflow!";
        this.writeLineActivity1.Name = "writeLineActivity1";
        this.Activities.Add(this.writeLineActivity1);
        this.Name = "MyWorkflow";

        this.CanModifyActivities = false;
    }
}
```

This code will look similar to the code created by the workflow designer in our first example of this chapter. The InitializeComponent method creates a tree of activities by creating a WriteLineActivity and adding the activity to the Activities collection. Notice the class also includes a partial keyword on the class definition. Remember, the partial keyword allows a class definition to span multiple source code files, and allows us to augment the compiler-generated code with our own code. We will revisit the implications of the partial class definition soon.

Not only can we generate source code from XAML, we can generate XAML from a workflow instance. Remember XAML is essentially an XML serialization format for managed objects. We can walk up to a workflow object with a `WorkflowMarkupSerializer` and produce mark-up. The following code will display the mark-up for a running workflow:

```
using (WorkflowRuntime runtime = new WorkflowRuntime())
using (StringWriter stream = new StringWriter())
using (XmlWriter writer = XmlWriter.Create(stream))
{
    Type t = typeof(MyWorkflow);
    WorkflowInstance instance = runtime.CreateWorkflow(t);

    WorkflowMarkupSerializer serializer;
    serializer = new WorkflowMarkupSerializer();

    serializer.Serialize(
        writer,
        instance.GetWorkflowDefinition()
    );

    Console.WriteLine(stream.ToString());
}
```

If we run this code on a workflow instance with our custom activity, we will produce the following XAML.

```
<?xml version="1.0" encoding="utf-8"?>
<ns0:MyWorkflow
    x:Name="MyWorkflow"
    xmlns:x="http://schemas.microsoft.com/winfx/2006/xaml"
    xmlns:ns0="clr-namespace:ReSerialize;Assembly=chapter2_Host"
/>
```

Notice the workflow definition is now opaque. When the workflow compiler creates a new type from a workflow definition, the definition becomes fixed and we cannot see the activities inside with serialization. We can still create an instance of the above workflow using XAML activation, which we will cover in the next section. XAML activation walks the XML and creates objects from the mark-up instructions. When activation instantiates `MyWorkflow`, the `InitializeComponent` method will create all the activities for the workflow, so the serialization does not need to explicitly list the child activities with XAML. The instance will work just like our other examples and execute a `WriteLineActivity`, thanks to the code the compiler generated for the `MyWorkflow` class.

XAML Activation

In some scenarios, compilation can become a burden. Imagine a database containing a thousand or more workflow definitions tailored and updated for specific users. In this scenario, we might want to avoid the churn of creating new assemblies. What we want to do is load and execute a workflow with the least amount of overhead. Fortunately, this is an area where a pure XAML approach excels, thanks to a feature known as XAML activation.

If we want to activate the workflow we created earlier, we have to tweak the XOML file. Remember we used an `x:Class` attribute to tell the compiler the name of the `Type` to create from the workflow definition. Since we will not be putting the XAML through a compilation phase, there is no compiler available to create a new class. Notice the XAML we created through the `WorkflowMarkupSerializer` earlier does not include an `x:Class` attribute.

```
<SequentialWorkflowActivity
  xmlns="http://schemas.microsoft.com/winfx/2006/xaml/workflow"
  xmlns:otc="http://schemas.OdeToCode.com/WinWF/Activities"
  >

  <otc:WriteLineActivity Message="Hello, workflow!"/>

</SequentialWorkflowActivity>
```

Activation is only available for workflows defined entirely in workflow mark-up. Since there is no compiler involved, we will need to give up features provided by the XAML namespace (including the ability to define in-line code). Activation merely creates an object hierarchy directly from the XAML representation. XAML is effectively an XML serialization format for CLR objects.

Activation takes place with the same `CreateWorkflow` method of the `WorkflowRuntime` class that we've used earlier. However, we need to use a different overload of the method. Instead of passing a `Type` object, we need to pass an `XmlReader` to steam our workflow mark-up into the runtime.

```
using (WorkflowRuntime runtime = new WorkflowRuntime())
using (AutoResetEvent waitHandle = new AutoResetEvent(false))
```

```
{
    runtime.WorkflowCompleted += delegate { waitHandle.Set(); };
    runtime.WorkflowTerminated += delegate { waitHandle.Set(); };

    TypeProvider typeProvider = new TypeProvider(runtime);
    typeProvider.AddAssembly(Assembly.GetExecutingAssembly());
    runtime.AddService(typeProvider);

    XmlReader reader = XmlReader.Create(@"..\..\purexaml\purexaml5.
xoml");
    WorkflowInstance instance = runtime.CreateWorkflow(reader);
    instance.Start();

    waitHandle.WaitOne();
}
```

When we were compiling XOML files, we could specify an assembly reference to the assembly containing our custom `WriteLineActivity`. When activating a workflow, the runtime will still need to locate custom activity assemblies, but this time we need to use a `TypeProvider` service. A `TypeProvider` holds references to assemblies needed for workflow activation. The runtime will rely on the `TypeProvider` service to resolve types and assemblies. In our code we are adding the executing assembly as an assembly reference.

One impact to consider before using activated workflows revolves around versioning. When we compile a workflow, we can provide an assembly version and other metadata to identify the assembly. We can even provide a strong name to uniquely identify the assembly and prevent tampering. XOML files, on the other hand, have no versioning infrastructure built in, so if we need versioning or cryptographic signing we'll have to write some custom code.

XAML-only Summary

We've covered the options available to build pure XAML solutions. Taking a pure XAML approach to building workflows can be useful if we want to use the workflow activation features for a lightweight approach to building new workflows. XAML is also a good approach when we build custom tools to define workflows, as these tools can rely on XML libraries and APIs to construct markup. A pure XAML approach doesn't work so well when we want to augment a workflow with our own C# or Visual Basic code. In the next section, we will take a look at combining XAML with code.

Code and XAML Together

Visual Studio offers a second option for building workflows. The second option uses XAML mark-up and **code separation**, also commonly referred to as **code-beside**. In this scenario, the designer stores mark-up inside a XOML file, and we augment the definition with source code in a C# or Visual Basic file. The item template for this option is **Sequential Workflow (with code separation)**.

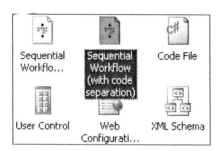

This item template also adds two files to the project. If we call our workflow `CodeSeparation`, the files will be `CodeSeparation.xoml`, and `CodeSeparation.xoml.cs`. If we build the same workflow as we did at the beginning of the chapter (with a `CodeActivity` inside), our `CodeSeparation.xoml.cs` file will look like the following:

```
using System;
using System.Workflow.Activities;

namespace chapter2_library
{
  public partial class CodeSeparation :
      SequentialWorkflowActivity
  {
      private void codeActivity1_ExecuteCode(object sender,

    EventArgs e)
      {

      }
    }
}
```

Our XOML file, meanwhile, contains the following XAML:

```
<SequentialWorkflowActivity
  x:Class="chapter2_library.CodeSeparation"
  x:Name="CodeSeparation"
  xmlns:x="http://schemas.microsoft.com/winfx/2006/xaml"
  xmlns="http://schemas.microsoft.com/winfx/2006/xaml/workflow">
```

```
<CodeActivity
  x:Name="codeActivity1"
  ExecuteCode="codeActivity1_ExecuteCode"
/>

</SequentialWorkflowActivity>
```

 The default editor for a XOML file is the graphical workflow designer. If we want to look at the XAML in a XOML file, we can right-click the file and select the **Open With** option. The **Open With** dialog will give us a choice of editors, including the XML editor, which let's us see and modify the XAML inside.

Remember the project file for our workflow project will include MSBuild targets, and these targets know how to compile XAML workflow definitions in XOML files. The workflow compiler will first generate C# source code into a file in a temporary directory. The file will contain a class named CodeSeparation and marked with the partial keyword modifier, which allows our partial CodeSeperation class to augment the workflow. We've reviewed this process earlier in the chapter. The C# compiler picks up the final class definition by using both files.

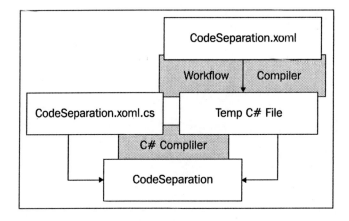

What we do not get to see in this process is the temporary C# code, but this code will look like the code we generated earlier with the workflow compiler and the /t:codegen parameter. Although we have not used our custom WriteLineActivity in any of the workflows designed with Visual Studio, the **Toolbox** window will contain the activity and allow us to drop the activity into the workflow. Visual Studio will automatically add any custom activities it finds in the current solution to the **Toolbox** window.

Summary

We've looked at several options available for authoring and building workflows. We've built workflows using XOML files and compiled the files both programmatically and from the command line. We also built workflow using pure code, and with code separation. When it comes time to execute a workflow, the result from each option is nearly the same. All the options ultimately produce a collection of objects in memory, and the objects maintain parent-child relationships. The workflow runtime manages the execution of the objects.

Code-based workflow definitions are perfectly reasonable to use for general-purpose, fixed workflows. When using the workflow designer, chances are we'll never have to look at the designer-generated code, and we don't particularly care if the designer is using XAML, C#, or Visual Basic code to maintain the workflow definition.

XAML-based workflow definitions open up a number of additional possibilities. If we have a workflow definition entirely in XAML we can use workflow activation and avoid compilation. Activation is useful when building a large number of dynamic workflows. We merely need to pass the XML into the workflow runtime to have a run-able instance of a workflow.

Using XAML with code-beside files will keep our workflow definition in an XML file. If we need to write custom tools for our workflows, like a custom workflow designer, then XAML is the preferred approach. XAML is both tool-able, and we can use the wide variety of existing XML APIs to build our tool. XAML, like the CLR, is also language agnostic. The XAML-based workflow can work equally well alongside any .NET language. Also, if we want to forego the graphical designer and tweak workflow definitions by hand, the XML format is easier to read and comprehend compared to a code-based definition.

3
Sequential Workflows

Windows Workflow offers two workflow execution styles out of the box: sequential and event-driven. A sequential workflow completes one activity and moves to the next, executing a sequence of consecutive steps. As an example, a sequential workflow could model the process of moving records from a website's compressed log file into a database table. Step 1 would download the compressed log file. Step 2 would decompress the log file. Step 3 would bulk insert records from the log file into a table, and step 4 would create summary statistics from the new records. Even though a sequential workflow can use branches, loops, and receive external events, it is mostly predictable and marches inevitably forward to completion.

Event-driven workflows, on the other hand, rely on external events to drive them to a finishing point. Event-driven workflows model a workflow as a state machine. A state machine consists of a set of states (including an initial state and a final state), and a set of events. The state machine is always in one of the defined states, and cannot transition to a new state until an event arrives.

With these differences in mind, let's explore sequential workflows, and return to state machines in Chapter 7.

The SequenceActivity

Activities are the basic building blocks in Windows Workflow, and a sequential workflow itself is an activity — a `SequentialWorkflowActivity` to be precise. The `SequentialWorkflowActivity` class derives from the `SequenceActivity` class, which in turn derives from the `CompositeActivity` class. These superclasses dictate the behavior and characteristics of a sequential workflow. The class diagram as shown on the next page depicts this class hierarchy.

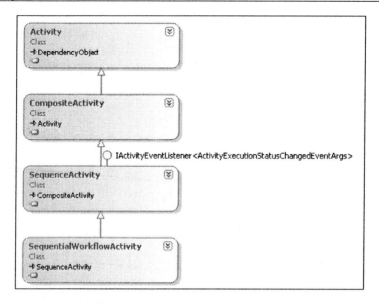

The `CompositeActivty` class provides the logic for an activity to contain one or more child activities. A sequential workflow will typically contain multiple children (and the children may also be `CompositeActivity` objects with their own children).

The `SequenceActivity` class provides the logic to execute child activities. The `SequenceActivity` iterates through its children in a forward-only direction, executing each child once and then moving to the next child. When the last child activity is complete, the sequence is finished. As we mentioned earlier, this doesn't mean a sequential activity cannot loop or branch, but it does mean execution always moves forward. There is no mechanism available to jump back to an arbitrary activity in the workflow.

Simple Flow

As an example, let's start building a simple sequential workflow. Our workflow will increment a counter and write the counter value to the screen. To start writing our workflow we will use the **Sequential Workflow Console Application** C# template from the Visual Studio **New Project** menu. The project wizard will give us an application and a workflow definition named `Workflow1`. Right-click on the workflow and select **View Code** to open the code-beside file. Inside, we'll place the highlighted code below:

```
public partial class Workflow1 : SequentialWorkflowActivity
{
    int counter = 0;
}
```

Back in the workflow design window, we'll drag a CodeActivity from the **Toolbox** window to the design surface. Sequential workflows and sequence activities in general always start execution at the top of the flow and end at the bottom. Drop points (small green plus signs) will appear along the line of execution whenever we are dragging an activity nearby. In the **Properties** window, we can give this activity a name of IncrementCounter. We'll drag a second CodeActivity from the **Toolbox** and drop the activity beneath our first activity. We'll give this activity the name of WriteCounter. Our workflow will look as below:

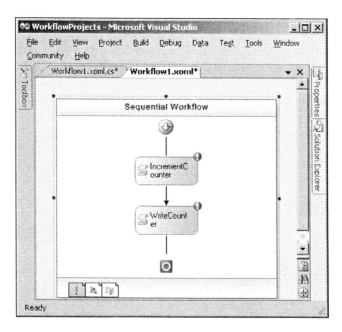

Next, we can give our IncrementCounter an ExecuteCode handler by double-clicking the activity in the workflow designer. The designer will generate a skeletal method for the handler, and all we have to do is supply the internal details. We'll add one line of code to increment the counter field.

```
private void IncrementCounter_ExecuteCode(object sender, EventArgs e)
{
    counter++;
}
```

We can return to the designer view, double-click WriteCounter, and add the following code:

```
private void WriteCounter_ExecuteCode(object sender, EventArgs e)
{
    Console.WriteLine("The value of counter is {0}.", counter);
}
```

If we run this workflow, we'll only see one line of output, telling us, **The value of counter is 1**. The sequential workflow executes the two child activities in the order they appear, and after both have executed, the sequential workflow is complete. Next, we'll add some control flow activities to make the workflow more interesting.

Sequences Inside Sequences

The WhileActivity allows us to execute a single child activity until a condition returns false. We can drag a WhileActivity from the **Toolbox** into our sequential workflow as the first activity in the workflow.

An empty WhileActivity will display **Drop An Activity Here** on the designer screen. It might sound surprising that we can place only a single child activity inside the WhileActivity. The WhileActivity derives from the CompositeActivity class, meaning it will hold child activities, but it isn't derived from SequenceActivity, which provides the logic to execute multiple child activities. Instead, the WhileActivity executes only a single child activity.

If we want both of our code activities to execute inside the WhileActivity, we need to enclose the activities inside a SequenceActivity. We can drag a SequenceActivity from the **Toolbox** and drop the activity inside the WhileActivity. Then we can move both of our code activities inside the sequence. Our workflow would now look as shown in the screenshot on the next page.

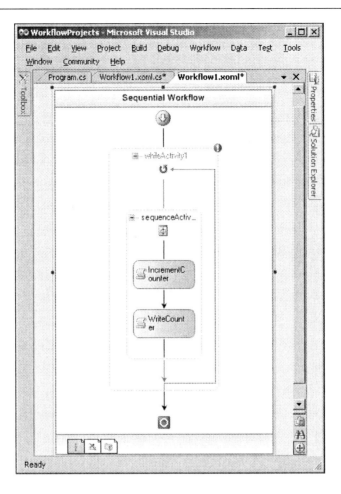

Before we can run the workflow, we'll need to provide a condition for the WhileActivity to evaluate. We can write conditions into an external rules file, or directly in code. Let's add the following method to the code behind the workflow:

```
private void CheckCounter(object sender, ConditionalEventArgs e)
{
    e.Result = false;
    if (counter < 10)
    {
        e.Result = true;
    }
}
```

The CheckCounter method is a special method known as a **code condition**. In WF, a code condition returns a true or false value through the Result property of a ConditionalEventArgs argument. In the **Properties** window for the WhileActivity, we can set **Condition** to **Code Condition**, and select `CheckCounter` in the drop-down list of available conditions. Now our workflow will print ten lines to the console, each with a higher value for the counter field.

Of course, not all workflows can run in isolation using only a counter field and the console. We often need to pass data to a workflow and fetch data from a workflow.

Workflows and the Outside World

For many workflows, an important step will be to decide how the workflow will interact with an application. How do we know if a workflow finished successfully or threw an exception? How do we get data into a workflow instance? When the workflow completes, how do we get data out? Technically, there are an infinite number of solutions to these questions. In this section, however, we are going to cover some of the fundamental techniques.

The basic mechanisms for communicating with a workflow include events, methods, and workflow parameters. An application can both raise events to a workflow instance and receive lifecycle events about a workflow instance from the workflow runtime. These lifecycle events are the first topic for discussion.

Workflow Instance Lifetime Events

The `WorkflowRuntime` class is the gateway to all running workflows. `WorkflowRuntime` exposes a number of events we can use to detect changes in a running workflow. These events are listed in the following table:

Name	Description
WorkflowAborted	Occurs when an instance aborts. The `WorkflowInstance` class includes an `Abort` method to abort a workflow.
WorkflowCompleted	Occurs when the instance completes, and includes a `WorkflowCompletedEventArgs` parameter to retrieve any output parameters.
WorkflowCreated	Occurs after we create a workflow with the WorkflowRuntime's `CreateWorkflow` method.
WorkflowIdled	Occurs when a workflow enters an idle state. A workflow becomes idle when it is waiting for a timer or external event to take place, for instance.
WorkflowLoaded	Occurs when a persistence service has restored a workflow instance into memory to continue execution.
WorkflowPersisted	Occurs when a persistence service persists a workflow. A workflow may persist and then unloaded from memory when it is in the idle state and waiting for an event.

Name	Description
WorkflowSuspended	Occurs when the runtime suspends a workflow, typically due to a `SuspendActivity` in the workflow.
WorkflowResumed	Occurs when workflow execution continues after a suspension.
WorkflowStarted	Occurs when a workflow firsts starts execution.
WorkflowTerminated	Occurs when a workflow terminates, typically due to an unhandled exception. `WorkflowTerminatedEventArgs` will include the exception object.
WorkflowUnloaded	Occurs when the runtime unloads a workflow from memory, typically due to the workflow being idle.

To see these events in action we can look at the project named `chapter3_sequential` in the code accompanying the book. The **WorkflowEvents.xoml** file in the project includes a Code activity and a Suspend activity. The design mode of the workflow should look as shown in the screenshot below:

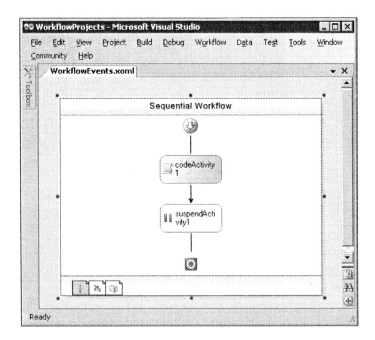

The Code activity in this workflow only writes a message to the console. The code behind **WorkflowEvents** is shown below:

```
using System;
using System.Workflow.Activities;

namespace chapter3_sequential
```

```
{
    public partial class WorkflowEvents : SequentialWorkflowActivity
    {
        private void codeActivity1_ExecuteCode(object sender,
                                                        EventArgs e)
        {
            Console.WriteLine("Executing...");
        }
    }
}
```

In `Program.cs`, the application wires up all of the `WorkflowRuntime` events using code like the following:

```
runtime.WorkflowCreated +=
    new EventHandler<WorkflowEventArgs>(runtime_WorkflowCreated);
runtime.WorkflowIdled +=
    new EventHandler<WorkflowEventArgs>(runtime_WorkflowIdled);
```

Each event handler writes a message to console, which enables us to see which events fire and when.

```
static void runtime_WorkflowIdled(object sender, WorkflowEventArgs e)
{
    Console.WriteLine("Workflow idled");
}

static void runtime_WorkflowCreated(object sender,
                                    WorkflowEventArgs e)
{
    Console.WriteLine("Workflow created");
}
```

Two of the events (`Terminated` and `Completed`) need to call the `Set` method of the program's `WaitHandle` object. As discussed in Chapter 1, the default runtime behavior is to execute our workflow on a background thread. The program will need to block the main thread on the `WaitHandle` object using the `WaitOne` method. The `WaitOne` method keeps the main thread waiting until the `Set` method signals completion of the workflow. If we didn't wait for the completion signal, the main thread would exit and the application would terminate before the workflow has a chance to execute.

Here is an event handler for the `Terminated` activity, which calls `Set` and writes information about the unhandled exception to the console.

```
static void runtime_WorkflowTerminated(object sender,
                                       WorkflowTerminatedEventArgs e)
```

```
    {
        Console.WriteLine("Workflow terminated");
        Console.WriteLine("\tException: " + e.Exception.Message);
        waitHandle.Set();
    }
```

Executing our console mode program produces the output shown in the screenshot below:

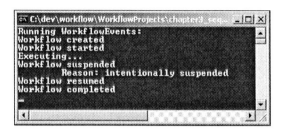

The output indicates that the workflow fired a **created** event, a **started** event, and then executed the code inside of the first CodeActivity. The next activity was the SuspendActivty highlighted in the screenshot below. The activity has an Error property available in the **Toolbox** window, and we've set this property to the string literal **intentionally suspended**.

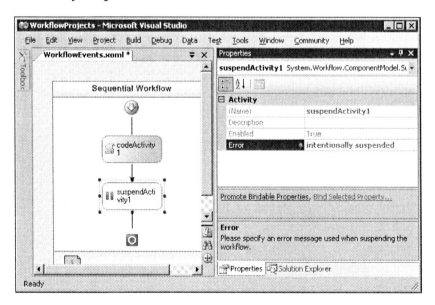

The suspendActivity tells the runtime to temporarily halt execution of the workflow instance. We might want to suspend a workflow if execution reaches a point where processing cannot continue without intervention, but we don't want to terminate the workflow with an exception. In this scenario, we are suspending the workflow just to see the `WorkflowSuspended` event fire. The contents of the `Error` property will be available to the event handler in an instance of the `WorkflowSuspendedEventArgs` class.

```
static void runtime_WorkflowSuspended(object sender,
                                WorkflowSuspendedEventArgs e)
{
    Console.WriteLine("Workflow suspended");
    Console.WriteLine("\tReason: " + e.Error);
    e.WorkflowInstance.Resume();
}
```

When the `WorkflowSuspended` event fires, we write out a message and immediately ask the workflow instance to resume processing. The workflow picks up where it left off, and runs to completion.

> Workflow instance events are not the only technique available for monitoring the execution of a workflow. A workflow **tracking service** can receive exceptionally granular information about the state of a workflow. WF provides a `SqlTrackingService` class to log tracking information to a SQL Server database, but we can also implement and plug a custom tracking service into the runtime. We cover tracking services in Chapter 6.

Of course, there will be times when we need to get information *into* a workflow before execution begins. Parameters are one technique for feeding data to a workflow.

Workflow Parameters

An overloaded version of the runtime's `CreateWorkflow` method allows us to pass parameters into a new workflow instance. Parameters are a collection of name and value pairs in an instance of the `Dictionary` generic class.

```
Dictionary<string, object> parameters = new Dictionary<string,
object>();
parameters.Add("FirstName", "Scott");
parameters.Add("LastName", "Allen");

instance = runtime.CreateWorkflow(typeof(WorkflowParameters),
parameters);
instance.Start();
```

When the workflow runtime creates a new workflow instance, it tries to find a **companion property** for each named parameter value. A companion property is a public, writable property on the workflow object with the same name as the parameter. For example, the following workflow class will accept incoming parameters with the names `FirstName` and `LastName`.

```
public partial class WorkflowParameters : SequentialWorkflowActivity
{
    public string FirstName
    {
        set { _firstName = value; }
    }
    private string _firstName;

    public string LastName
    {
        set { _lastName = value; }
    }
    private string _lastName;

    public string FullName
    {
        get { return _fullName; }
    }
    private string _fullName;

    private void codeActivity1_ExecuteCode(object sender,
                                           EventArgs e)
    {
        _fullName = String.Format("{0} {1}", _firstName, _lastName);
    }
    // ...
```

If we try to pass a `FullName` parameter, the runtime will throw an exception. The `FullName` property is a read-only property. If the runtime cannot find a public, writable companion property for an incoming parameter, it throws a `System.ArgumentException` exception. The reverse is not true, however. Parameters are optional, and we don't need to specify an input parameter for every public writable property.

The activities inside of a workflow don't need to perform any special tricks to fetch the parameter values. The runtime will have placed all the parameters into properties before execution begins. In the above code, we have an ExecuteCode event handler for a `CodeActivity` concatenating the backing fields for the first and last name parameters into a full name field. As you might have guessed, we will be able to retrieve the `FullName` property as an output parameter.

When a workflow completes, the runtime raises a `WorkflowCompleted` event and passes along a `WorkflowCompletedEventArgs` object. `WorkflowCompletedEventArgs` contains an `OutputParameters` property, which is a `Dictionary` collection of all output parameters. The runtime will copy the value of each public, readable workflow property into the `OutputParameters` collection.

```
static void runtime_WorkflowCompleted(object sender,
                                      WorkflowCompletedEventArgs e)
{
    Console.WriteLine("Workflow completed");
    Console.WriteLine("\tOutput parameters: ");

    foreach (KeyValuePair<string, object> pair in e.OutputParameters)
    {
        Console.WriteLine("\t\tName: {0} Value: {1}", pair.Key,
                                                      pair.Value);
    }

    waitHandle.Set();
}
```

The output of the above code will look as shown below:

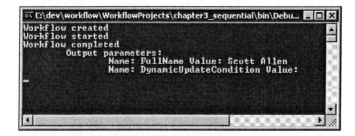

Raising Events and Invoking Methods

Many developers will want to establish a more formal mechanism for interacting with a workflow. Although the `Dictionary` approach is an easy and flexible approach to putting data into a workflow, it's easy to forget a parameter, or forget the name of a parameter. Also, we can only put data into a workflow using parameters at the *start* of a workflow, and only get data out at the end. Many workflows will need to exchange data with the host at various times during execution. To achieve this goal we can use events and method calls. This section is going to discuss the fundamentals of communication for data transfer, and we will return with more depth in Chapter 8.

Service Contracts

A workflow and its host can exchange data via a **local communication service (LCS)**. An LCS allows events and method calls between a workflow and a host. Behind the scenes, the workflow runtime works with an LCS to intercept communications and provide additional services (like queuing an event until a workflow is in a state to accept the event).

Communication via an LCS requires a messaging contract, and in .NET, a contract is synonymous with an interface. Interfaces will define the events and methods that an LCS will expose. Events pass data from the host to a workflow, while methods pass data from a workflow to the host. As an example, the following interface defines a bug tracking service with one event and one method:

```
[ExternalDataExchange]
interface IBugFlowService
{
    void AssignBug(Bug bug);
    event EventHandler<BugAddedArgs> BugAdded;
}
```

The workflow can invoke the `AssignBug` method to pass a `Bug` object to its host. Likewise, the host can raise the `BugAdded` event and pass data into a workflow via an event argument. The `ExternalDataExchange` attribute will identify this interface as a messaging contract. Windows Workflow will look for this piece of metadata when we add local services to the runtime. The `Bug` class we are passing is a simple data container with three properties, and looks like the following:

```
[Serializable]
public class Bug
{
    public Bug(int id, string title, string description)
    {
        _id = id;
        _title = title;
        _description = description;
    }
    public Bug()
    {

    }

    private int _id;
    public int ID
    {
        get { return _id; }
```

```
            set {  _id = value; }
        }

        private string _title;
        public string Title
        {
            get { return _title; }
            set { _title = value; }
        }

        private string _description;
        public string Description
        {
            get { return _description; }
            set { _description = value; }
        }
    }
```

All objects passing between a workflow and a host must be serializable objects. For the Bug class, we decorate the class with a Serializable attribute. In order to pass a Bug via an event, we will need a serializable event argument class, shown below:

```
    [Serializable]
    public class BugAddedArgs : ExternalDataEventArgs
    {
        public BugAddedArgs(Guid instanceId, Bug newBug)
            : base(instanceId)
        {
            _bug = newBug;
        }

        private Bug _bug;
        public Bug NewBug
        {
            get { return _bug; }
            set { _bug = value; }
        }
    }
```

In addition to being serializable, LCS events must derive from the ExternalDataEventArgs class (shown in the screenshot on the next page). The workflow runtime and the LCS will use additional properties provided by this class during event processing. One such property is the InstanceId, which we need to pass into the base class constructor. The InstanceId is a Globally Unique Identifier (**GUID**), and every workflow instance the runtime creates receives a unique instance identifier. The InstanceId will allow the runtime to route the events to the proper workflow instance.

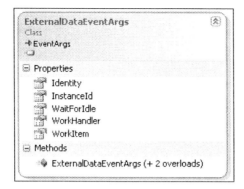

So far, we have defined three entities:

1. An `IBugFlowService` interface, which defines the communications allowed between host and workflows.

2. A `Bug` class, which holds the data we will pass back and forth.

3. A `BugAddedArgs` class, which derives from `ExternalDataEventArgs` and carries data to the workflow during the `BugAdded` event.

Now, we need to provide a concrete implementation of the service described by the contract.

Service Implementation

There is nothing particularly special about our local service implementation. The service merely needs to provide an appropriate implementation for the `IBugFlowService` interface. The service will be an intermediary between the host and bug tracking workflows.

```
public class BugFlowService : IBugFlowService
{
    public void AssignBug(Bug bug)
    {
        // notify someone that it is time to assign a bug...
        Console.WriteLine("Assign '{0}' to a developer", bug.Title);
    }

    public void CreateBug(Guid instanceID, Bug bug)
    {
        // tell the workflow about the new bug
        BugAddedArgs args = new BugAddedArgs(instanceID, bug);
        args.WaitForIdle = true;
        EventHandler<BugAddedArgs> ev = BugAdded;
        if (ev != null)
```

```
            ev(null, args);
    }

    public event EventHandler<BugAddedArgs> BugAdded;
}
```

In this example, our `AssignBug` method only prints a message to the console. In a real application, we might ultimately display a dialog box for a user to assign the bug (and then possibly raise another event to let the workflow know we've assigned a bug to a team member). The `CreateBug` method builds a `BugAddedArgs` object and raises the `BugAdded` event. The `WaitForIdle` property ensures the workflow will be in a state to receive the event. Now that we've implemented our messaging service, we can build a workflow to interact with the service.

Workflow Implementation

In this scenario, the two key activities from the base activity library are the `HandleExternalEventActivity` and the `CallExternalMethodActivity`. In the screenshot below, we've placed one of each activity into the workflow to communicate with the host application.

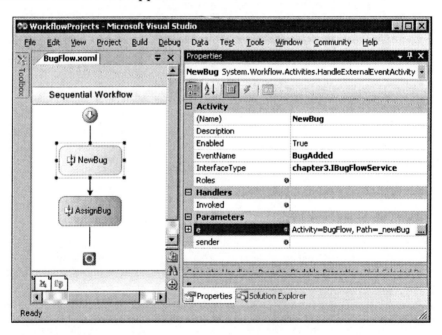

The first activity in the workflow is the `HandleExternalEventActivity`. In the **Properties** window, we configure the activity to listen for the `BugAdded` event by first setting **Interface Type** to our `IBugFlowService` contract (the full `Type` name, including namespace, is `chapter3.IBugFlowService`). We can then select `BugAdded`

for the **EventName** property. The **Parameters** section of the **Properties** windows allows us to bind the incoming `BugAddedArgs` parameter to a field in our workflow class. The event handling method uses the typical `sender` and `e` parameters to represent incoming event arguments.

Clicking the ellipsis in the screen opposite will display a dialog box where we can bind the parameter to an existing public field or property, or create a new field or property. The dialog box is shown below:

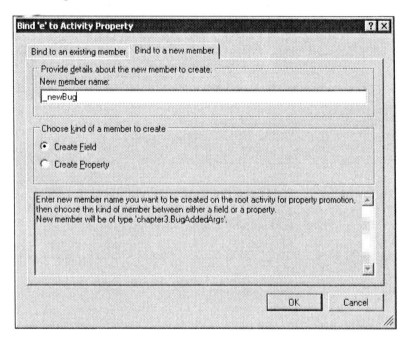

The next activity is the `CallExternalMethod` activity. Once again, we will use the **Properties** window to set the **Interface Type** property to our `IBigFlowService` interface, and tell the designer what method we want to invoke by selecting `AssignBug` for the **MethodName**. The `AssignBug` method needs a parameter, so we will click the ellipsis in the text box for the **bug** parameter, and create a new field with the name of `_bugToAssign`.

We are also going to generate an event handler for the activity's `MethodInvoking` event. We can do this by placing the cursor inside the text box on the `MethodInvoking` line and clicking the **Generate Handlers** link in the bottom of the **Properties** window. The designer will create an event handler in the class behind our workflow. The activity will fire this event just before calling the external method, and inside the event handler we can prepare the data we want to exchange. The screenshot on the next page displays the complete configuration for the `CallExternalMethodActivity`, which we have named `AssignBug`.

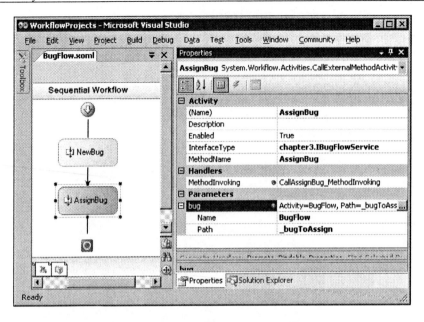

Finally, the following source code is all of the code-behind for our workflow, including the MethodInvoking event handler. Inside the handler, we copy the Bug reference from inside the _newBug field to the _bugToAssign field.

```
namespace chapter3_sequential
{
  public partial class BugFlow : SequentialWorkflowActivity
  {
        public chapter3.BugAddedArgs _newBug;
        public chapter3.Bug _bugToAssign;

        private void CallAssignBug_MethodInvoking(object sender,
                                                  EventArgs e)
        {
            _bugToAssign = _newBug.NewBug;
        }
    }
}
```

Remember the _newBug field is the field where the HandleExternalEventActivity placed the incoming data. We could have also bound the CallExternalMethodActivity parameter directly to the NewBug property of _newBug instead of creating a second field and using a MethodInvoking event handler.

Host Implementation

Finally, we need to write a host to execute our workflow.

```
WorkflowRuntime runtime = new WorkflowRuntime();

runtime.WorkflowCompleted +=
    new EventHandler<WorkflowCompletedEventArgs>(
        runtime_WorkflowCompleted);

runtime.WorkflowTerminated +=
    new EventHandler<WorkflowTerminatedEventArgs>(
        runtime_WorkflowTerminated);

ExternalDataExchangeService dataService;
dataService = new ExternalDataExchangeService();
runtime.AddService(dataService);

BugFlowService bugFlow = new BugFlowService();
dataService.AddService(bugFlow);

WorkflowInstance instance;
instance = runtime.CreateWorkflow(typeof(BugFlow));
instance.Start();

Bug bug = new Bug(1, "Bug Title", "Bug Description");
bugFlow.CreateBug(instance.InstanceId, bug);

waitHandle.WaitOne();
```

Here are the steps we are taking in the host program:

1. The host creates an `ExternalDataExchangeService` and adds the service to the workflow runtime. This service, provided by Windows Workflow, facilitates and manages all local communication services inside the workflow runtime, and will serve as the container for our own `BugFlowService`.

2. The host creates an instance of the `BugFlowService` and adds the service to the list of services managed by the data exchange service. The data exchange service will find the `IBugFlowService` interface, and prepare to handle `BugAdded` events and `AssignBug` method calls.

3. The host creates an instance of the `BugFlow` workflow, and starts the instance running. The workflow instance will wait for a `BugAdded` event.

4. The host creates a new `Bug` object, and passes the bug to the `bugFlow`'s `CreateBug` method.

At this point, we will turn to the visual depiction of the proceedings. The `CreateBug` method in our service will raise the `BugAdded` event. The workflow runtime (with help from the data exchange service) will catch the event, perform some processing, and pass the event to the workflow instance. The workflow instance might have been waiting for minutes, hours, days, or even months for this event to arrive, so we can't fire an event directly to the workflow instance. The workflow might not even be in memory at the time we raise the event; the runtime might have persisted the workflow into the database for long-term storage. By intercepting the event, the workflow runtime has the chance to load the workflow into memory before passing the event along. When the workflow calls the `AssignBug` method, it takes a direct route to our local service, although workflow does have the opportunity to perform some pre- and post-processing on the method call.

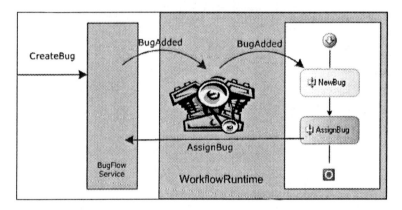

Faults

Of course, a workflow might not execute flawlessly. Unexpected exceptions may arise because a database server might not be available, for instance. We can also intentionally raise an exception with a `ThrowActivity`.

Managing exceptions inside a workflow is similar to managing exceptions in Visual Basic or C#. Composite activities can include **fault handlers** to *catch* exceptions. If an activity does not handle an exception that occurs, the runtime will let the exception propagate to the parent activity. This is similar to an exception moving up the call stack until the .NET runtime can locate an appropriate exception handler. If the runtime does not find a catch handler for a .NET application thread, the application terminates. If an exception occurs inside a workflow, and the runtime can find no fault handler to catch the exception, the runtime terminates the workflow and raises the `WorkflowTerminated` event.

The `FaultHandlerActivity` handles exceptions in Windows Workflow. We can view the fault handlers for a composite activity by right-clicking the activity and selecting **View Faults**. The designer for a sequential workflow activity includes a shortcut at the bottom of the designer screen. The third small page icon from the left is the view fault shortcut, which will display the screen as shown below:

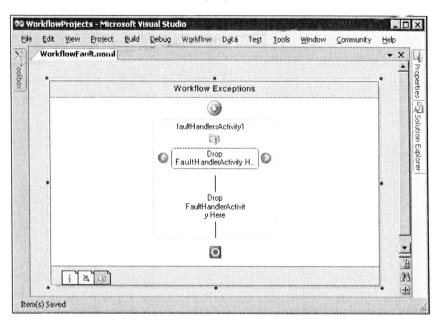

Inside the fault view is a storyboard where we can drop one or more `FaultHandlerActivity` shapes. We will associate each `FaultHandlerActivity` with a .NET exception type, such as `System.NullReferenceException` or `System.ArgumentException`. Just like catch clauses in Visual Basic and C#, a fault handler will handle any exceptions of the given type, or any exceptions derived from the given type. In the following screenshot, overleaf, we've added a fault handler with a **FaultType** of `System.Exception`. Since every exception ultimately derives from `System.Exception`, this fault handler will handle any possible exception in the workflow.

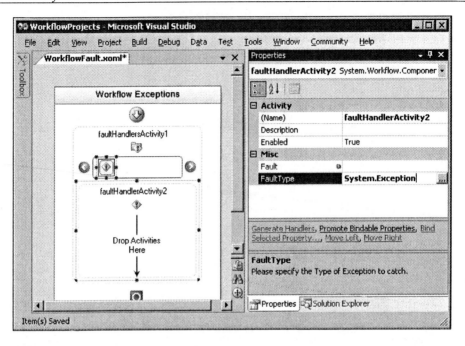

Each fault handler can have a list of child activities to execute when it catches an exception. Just like exception handlers in a general-purpose programming language, the purpose of a fault handler is to clean up or reverse any partially completed work. The workflow runtime will raise the `WorkflowCompleted` event if the `SequentialWorkflowActivity` fault handler handles an exception, as opposed to raising the `WorkflowTerminated` event if the exception goes unhandled. If we want to make sure the workflow terminates, we can use a `ThrowActivity` inside the fault handler.

In the screenshot on the next page, we've set up a fault handler with the following configuration:

- The fault handler specifies a `FaultType` of `System.Exception`. The activity binds the incoming exception to a member field with the name of `fault`.

- The first child activity, a `CodeActivity`, will write a message to the console about the exception.

- The second child activity, a `ThrowActivity`, will re-throw the handled exception by specifying the `Fault` as mapping to the `fault` field.

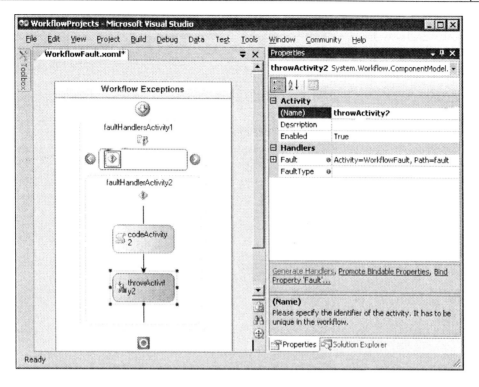

Summary

In this chapter we've explored some of the details of the `SequentialWorkflowActivity`, including how to communicate and pass data between a sequential workflow and its host, and how to handle faults inside a sequence of activities.

Sequential workflows inherit most of their behavior from the `SequenceActivity` class, which can appear in more than just a sequential workflow. As we will see later in the book, sequential activities are also important in the other primary type of workflow, the event-driven workflow.

4

The Base Activity Library

Activities are the basic building blocks for workflows. The base activity library in Windows Workflow contains general-purpose activities to use for all workflows. There are activities for control flow, transaction management, local communication, web services, and more. These activities appear on the **Toolbox** window of the workflow designer. Some of these activities, like the CodeActivity, are simple. The job of the CodeActivity is to execute a block of code. Other activities, like the PolicyActivity, are more complex. The PolicyActivity can evaluate prioritized rules with forward chaining. We can build powerful workflows using just the activities inside the base activity library.

We are about to embark on a tour of the base activity library. Many of the activities here deserve a more thorough coverage, but our goal for this tour is to understand the basic capabilities of each activity type, and come away with an idea of when we can use each one. We will start the tour with the most basic activities.

The Basics

These activities model primitive operations that exist in almost every programming environment, such as conditional branching, looping, and grouping of sub-activities. We will start with an activity that appears many times in these code samples, the CodeActivity.

The CodeActivity

The Code activity's only interesting feature is its ExecuteCode event. We will need to pair the event with an event handler before the activity will pass validation. In the workflow designer, we can double-click on a Code activity, and Visual Studio will create and assign the event handler for us — all we need to do is write the code. The following code is an event handler for ExecuteCode that displays a message on the screen.

```
private void codeActivity1_ExecuteCode(object sender, EventArgs e)
{
    Console.WriteLine("Hello, world!");
}
```

The screenshot below shows a `Code` activity as it appears in the designer. A red exclamation point hovers above the top right of the activity because we have not assigned an `ExecuteCode` event handler, and the activity is failing validation. Any time an exclamation point appears, we can click with the mouse to find the reason for the validation error.

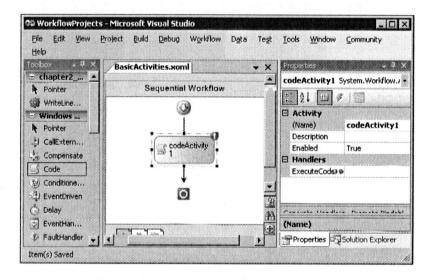

It might seem useful to execute arbitrary code in a workflow, but in reality the `Code` activity should appear relatively infrequently and as a special case. Instead of using `Code` activities, we should look to package code into custom activities (a topic for Chapter 5). Custom activities can expose properties and allow us to turn arbitrary code into a reusable activity.

Also, many of the activities we will examine raise events when they execute. We can use the handlers for these events to write small pieces of customized code to perform small tasks instead of dropping a new `Code` activity into the workflow. We will see an example of these event handlers soon.

The IfElseActivity

The `IfElse` activity is similar to the If…Then…Else statement in Visual Basic, and the if-else in C#. Inside an `IfElse` activity are one or more `IfElseBranch` activities. Each branch activity has a `Condition` property. We are required to set the `Condition` property on all branches, except for the last branch.

The `IfElse` activity evaluates branches from left to right. The *first* branch whose condition property evaluates to true will execute. If no branches have a condition that evaluates to true, then no branches will execute. If the last branch has no condition assigned, it will execute (but only if no other branches executed).

We can add additional branches by right-clicking the `IfElseActivity` and selecting **Add Branch**. We can remove branches by right-clicking a branch and selecting **Delete**. The screenshot below shows an `IfElse` activity in action.

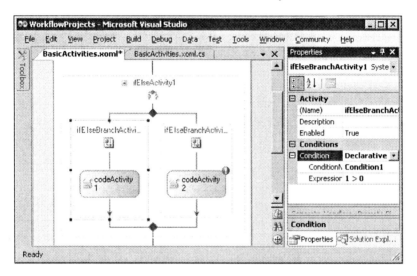

The `Condition` property of each branch can be configured as a declarative rule (which the designer persists to an external `.rules` file in XML format), or as a code condition (an event handler). If we configure the condition as a declarative rule, then we can launch the **Rule Condition Editor** from the **Properties** window and type an expression. For instance, if the workflow has an integer property named `Sales`, we could enter an expression like the following:

```
this.Sales > 10000
```

The same condition written as a `Code` condition would look like the following code:

```
private void checkSalesAmount(object sender, ConditionalEventArgs e)
{
    e.Result = Sales > 10000;
}
```

The activity raises an event to evaluate a `Code` condition. We can return the outcome of the condition as a true or false value in the event argument's `Result` property. In the **Properties** window, we can set the name of the `Code` condition to the name of this method (`checkSalesAmount`). Chapter 9 will cover conditions in more detail.

The WhileActivity

Like the IfElse activity, the While activity has a Condition property that can be either a declarative rule or a code condition. The WhileActivity will continue to run as long as the condition returns true. This activity will evaluate its condition *before* each iteration.

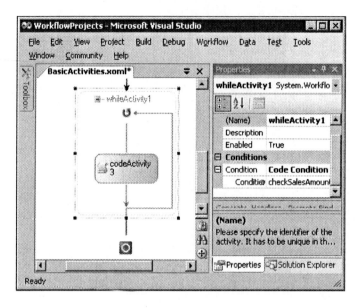

Unlike the IfElseBranchActivity, the WhileActivity can hold only a single child activity inside. This restriction doesn't prevent us from using multiple activities inside a loop, as we will see in the next section.

The SequenceActivity

A Sequence activity is a composite activity, and will manage one or more child activities. The activities inside a sequence execute one at a time, until the last activity completes. The WhileActivity only permits a single child activity, but if we make the single activity a SequenceActivity, we can drop additional activities inside the sequence activity. All of the children will then run sequentially each time the WhileActivity completes an iteration.

The SuspendActivity

The Suspend activity will temporarily halt a workflow. A Suspend activity might be useful when a workflow encounters an error that requires manual intervention. The activity has an Error property, which is a string.

A host can subscribe to the workflow runtime's `WorkflowSuspended` event and retrieve the error message using the `Error` property of the event's `WorkflowSuspendedEventArgs` parameter. The event argument also exposes a `WorkflowInstance` property. A host can resume execution of the workflow using the `Resume` method of the `WorkflowInstance` class, or bring about a sad and early ending with the `Terminate` method.

The TerminateActivity

Like the `Suspend` activity, the `Terminate` activity will halt the execution of a workflow. Unlike a suspended workflow, a host cannot resume a terminated workflow. We can use this activity if a workflow reaches a point where it cannot continue and has no hope of recovery.

The `Terminate` activity has an `Error` property of type string. A host can subscribe to the runtime's `WorkflowTerminated` event and examine the error. The event handler will receive an argument of type `WorkflowTerminatedEventArgs`, and the runtime will wrap the error message into a `WorkflowTerminatedException`, which is available through the argument's `Exception` property.

If we want a specific exception to arrive in the `WorkflowTerminated` event handler, we should use a `Throw` activity instead of a `Terminate` activity. However, there is a chance that the workflow can catch a thrown exception and continue, while the `Terminate` activity will always bring execution to a crashing halt.

The ThrowActivity

The `Throw` activity is similar to the throw statements in C# and Visual Basic — the activity raises an exception. Why should we use a `Throw` activity when we could throw from the `ExecuteCode` event of a `Code` activity? Because using a `Throw` activity makes the exception an explicit piece of the workflow model.

If the exception goes unhandled and propagates out of the workflow, the WF runtime will catch the exception, terminate the workflow, and raise the `WorkflowTerminated` event. The runtime will make the exception available in the `WorkflowTerminated` event arguments. The `Fault` property of this activity will reference the exception to throw. We can data-bind the `Fault` property to a field in our workflow, or to the property of another activity.

We can use the `FaultType` property to describe and restrict the exception types the activity will throw. If the `FaultType` is not set, the activity can throw any type of exception (as long as the type is `System.Exception`, or derived from there).

The InvokeWorkflowActivity

The `InvokeWorkflow` activity will asynchronously execute another workflow. Since the execution is asynchronous, we cannot retrieve output parameters from the other workflow, although we could set up additional communication mechanisms with the host to make the output available.

In the designer, we set the `TargetWorkflow` property to reference the workflow type we wish to execute. We can choose from workflow types defined in the same project, or in a referenced assembly. Once we've set the target, the designer will allow us to set up parameter bindings by looking at the public properties of the target type. We can bind fields and properties of our workflow as parameters for the target workflow. Before starting the second workflow, this activity will fire an `Invoking` event. We can use code inside the `Invoking` event handler to tweak and initialize the parameters.

We can use the `InvokeWorkflow` activity to kick off workflows that execute independently. For example, a workflow for a software bug tracking system might need to spin off workflows for regression testing and integration testing each time a new software build arrives.

The ParallelActivity

The `Parallel` activity allows multiple activities to execute at the same time. This does not mean the `Parallel` activity permits parallel processing across multiple threads *only a single thread will execute inside a workflow*. Instead, the `Parallel` activity allows separate branches inside the activity to execute independently.

As an example, let's pretend we are writing a workflow that requires a yes or no vote from three members of our company: the chief executive officer (CEO), the chief technology officer (CTO), and the chief financial officer (CFO). The host will deliver the votes to the workflow as events. We saw in the last chapter how the `HandleExternalEvent` activity can wait on events from a local communication service, so we will design our workflow to use three `HandleExternalEvent` activities.

We could write the workflow so that it would wait for the votes to arrive sequentially — first the CEO, then the CTO, then the CFO. This means the CTO couldn't vote until the CEO cast a vote, and the CFO couldn't vote until the CTO cast a vote. If the CTO is away for a few days and can't vote, the CFO will have to wait. A word of advice from the author — making a CFO unhappy does not increase your chances of career advancement at the company.

If the order of the votes is not important, it would make sense to let the software collect the votes as they arrive — in any order. The `Parallel` activity as shown in the screenshot below will listen for all three events simultaneously. Whichever officer votes first, the workflow will process the event and then wait for the other two events to arrive. The `Parallel` activity will not finish until all branches are finished processing (in this scenario, all three events must arrive).

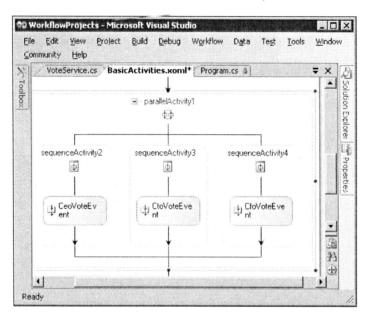

The DelayActivity

The `Delay` activity will initialize a timer and wait for the timer to expire. The `Delay` activity is often used to model a time-out, as it returns control to the workflow engine and allows other activities to execute while waiting for the timer. The `TimeoutDuration` property is a `TimeSpan` that represents the amount of time to wait. We can initialize the property in the designer, or programmatically by assigning an event handler for the `InitializeTimeoutDuration`, shown below:

```
private void delayActivity1_InitializeTimeoutDuration(
          object sender, EventArgs e)
{
   DelayActivity delay = sender as DelayActivity;
   if (delay != null)
   {
      // a 5 second time span
      delay.TimeoutDuration = new TimeSpan(0, 0, 5);
   }
}
```

We often find a `Delay` activity inside a `Listen` activity.

The ListenActivity

Like the `Parallel` activity, the `Listen` activity can contain multiple branches. Unlike the `Parallel` activity, the goal of a `Listen` activity is to finish *just one* branch. The branches of a `Listen` activity are `EventDriven` activities, and must start by the branches by waiting for an event (the first child must implement the `IEventActivity` interface). We'll see the `EventDriven` activity in more detail when we cover state machine workflows.

Let's go back to our previous workflow example with the CEO, the CTO, and the CFO. Previously we needed a vote from all three officers before the workflow could continue. If we only needed a vote from *one* of the three officers, the `Listen` activity would be a better fit. When one of the events arrives, the activity will execute the branch associated with the event and cancel the execution of the other branches.

As alluded to earlier, we can use a `Delay` activity inside a `Listen` activity to simulate a timeout. This arrangement is shown in the screenshot below. If the delay timer expires before any of the other events arrive, we can take an alternative action, perhaps by emailing a reminder to vote, or moving ahead with a default choice. Silence is consent!

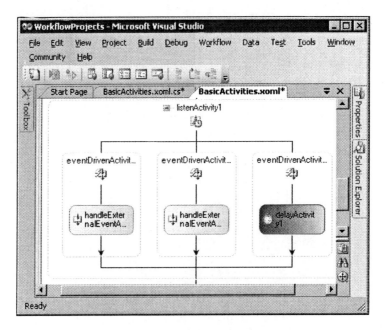

The EventHandlingScopeActivity

The EventHandlingScope activity is similar to a Listen activity in that it can have multiple branches waiting for events in parallel. We can view these branches by right-clicking the activity and selecting **View Events**. The primary difference between this activity and a Listen activity is that this event continues to listen for all events until the main child activity (the default view) finishes execution.

Imagine we are setting up a workflow that will count employee votes over a period of 30 minutes. We could set the main child activity of the EventHandlingScope activity as a Delay activity, with a 30-minute timeout. We can then place event handling activities in the event branches that listen for yes and no votes. This activity will continue to process the yes and no events until the Delay activity completes.

The SynchronizationScopeActivity

Like the threading synchronization primitives in the .NET libraries, the SynchronizationScope activity can serialize access to shared resources, even across workflow instances. If we have a static (C#) or shared (Visual Basic) field in our workflow definition, the SynchronizationScope can ensure only a single instance will have read and write access to the field for the duration of the activity.

The SynchronizationHandles property contains the handles that the workflow will acquire before it executes, and release upon completion. A synchronization handle is a simple string object, and the property maintains a collection of strings. Internally, the WF runtime will use each string as the key to a dictionary of locks. If the activity cannot acquire all the locks specified by the handles, it will wait until it can acquire the locks.

The ReplicatorActivity

The Replicator activity is similar to the While activity, but more sophisticated. The Replicator can process a collection of data either sequentially or in parallel, depending on the setting of the ExecutionType property. Think back to the example we talked about for the Parallel activity. We needed a vote from exactly *three* officers of the company before the workflow could proceed. The Replicator is a better fit when we don't know how many events we need to process until run time. Perhaps a user is checking off the required voters from a company-wide directory. A Replicator can create the required number of event listeners we need from the user's list of voters.

The InitialChildData property will hold the list of data objects for the Replicator to process. The Replicator will create a clone of its child activity to process each item in the child data collection. The Replicator will not finish execution until all the children have finished; however, there is an UntilCondition property that the Replicator will evaluate before starting, and after completion of each child. If the UntilCondition returns true, the Replicator will stop, even if it leaves children unprocessed. Like other conditions in WF, the UntilCondition can be a rule condition or a code condition.

The Replicator fires a number of useful events, including Initialized, Completed, ChildInitialized, and ChildCompleted. The ChildInitialized event is a good time to populate the cloned child activity with the data it needs to execute.

Local Communication Events

When it comes time for a workflow to communicate with the outside world, there are a handful of built-in activities to do the job. The activities we discuss in this section will communicate with local services provided by the hosting process.

For local communication to work, we need to define a contract in the form of a .NET interface. The interface will define the methods that a workflow can invoke on a local service, and the events that a local service can raise to a workflow.

Let's say we are working on a workflow for a bug-tracking system. At some point, a bug might need detailed information, like a screenshot, uploaded to the application. If the workflow needs this additional documentation, the workflow can ask the host to upload the document. The host might upload the documents itself, but more than likely it will notify a user that the bug requires more information. In either case, the workflow will have to wait (perhaps a few seconds, perhaps a few days or longer), for the uploaded document to arrive. The host can let the workflow know when the upload is complete via an event. The following interface defines the communication contract we need to enable this scenario. The ExternalDataExchange attribute is required for local communication services and aids the WF runtime in identifying this interface as a service contract.

```
[ExternalDataExchange]
interface IBugService
{
    bool RequestUpload(Guid id, string userName);
    event EventHandler<UploadCompletedEventArgs> UploadCompleted;
}
```

The two activities that interact with the interface are the CallExternalMethodActivity and HandleExternalEventActivity.

The CallExternalMethodActivity

The `CallExternalMethod` activity invokes a method on a local service. All we need to do is set up the properties of the activity, as shown in the screenshot below:

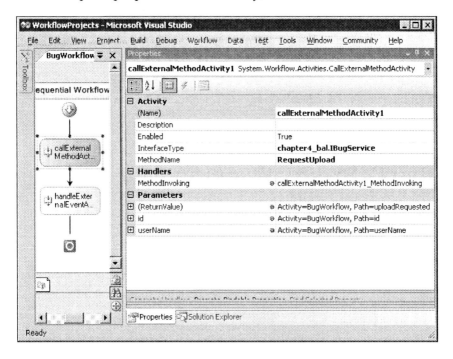

The `InterfaceType` property should be set first, as this will allow the designer to discover the available methods on the service. Once we set `InterfaceType` to the interface we defined, we can select the method to call in the `MethodName` property. The designer will then populate the **Parameters** area of the **Properties** window. We can bind all the input parameters, and the method return value, to fields and properties in our workflow. The `uploadRequested`, `id`, and `userName` fields are all member variables in the code-behind class of the workflow.

For the `CallExternalMethod` activity to work, we will need to add the `ExternalDataExchangeService` to the workflow runtime, and add a service that implements our interface to the data exchange service, as shown in the code below. The `BugFlowService` class implements the `IBugService` interface.

```
WorkflowRuntime workflowRuntime = new WorkflowRuntime();
ExternalDataExchangeService dataService = new
ExternalDataExchangeService();
workflowRuntime.AddService(dataService);
```

```
BugFlowService bugService = new BugFlowService();
dataService.AddService(bugService);
```

The `CallExternalMethod` activity includes a `MethodInvoking` event. The event will fire just before the activity calls the external method, and gives us an opportunity to set up the parameters. We might add code like the following to the event:

```
private void callExternalMethodActivity1_MethodInvoking(
    object sender, EventArgs e)
{
    id = this.WorkflowInstanceId;
    userName = "Scott";
}
```

The HandleExternalEventActivity

The `HandleExternalEvent` activity, like the `CallExternalMethod` activity, has an `InterfaceType` property we must set. Once we have set this property we can set the `EventName` property (see the screenshot below).

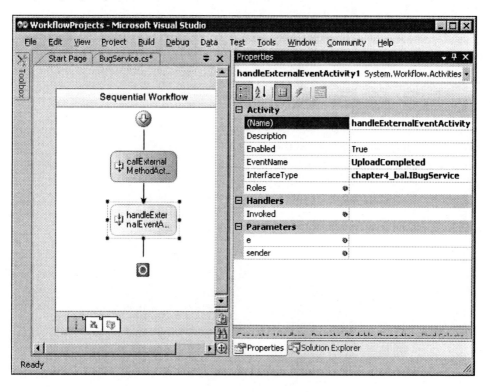

`HandleExternalEvent` is a blocking activity, meaning the activity is not going to complete until the event arrives from a local service. If there is a chance the event will never arrive, or if the event needs to arrive within a span of time, then it's best to use this activity inside a `ListenActivity`. As we described earlier, the `Listen` activity has multiple branches, and we can place a `DelayActivity` in one of the branches to simulate a timeout.

The `Roles` property of this activity can bind to a `WorkflowRoleCollection` object and allow the runtime to perform role-based authorization checks. The runtime compares the role memberships of the incoming identity against the allowable roles defined in the collection. The collection holds objects derived from the abstract `WorkflowRole` class. WF provides two concrete implementations of `WorkflowRole` with the `ActiveDirectoryRole` and `WebWorkflowRole` classes. These classes work with Active Directory and ASP.NET 2.0 Role Providers, respectively. If authorization fails, the runtime will throw a `WorkflowAuthorizationException` exception.

The Activity Generator

When working with local communication services, it's often a good idea to make use of the activity generator. Windows Workflow includes a command-line tool called the Windows Workflow Communications Activity Generator. This tool runs from the command line, and you can find it in the WF install directory with the name of `wca.exe`.

We can pass `wca.exe` the path to a .NET assembly (`.dll`), and the tool will look through the assembly for interfaces decorated with the `ExternalDataExchange` attribute. When the tool finds such an interface it will generate dedicated custom activities for calling the methods and handling the events of the interface.

For our `IBugService` interface, the tool will generate a `RequestUploadActivity` and an `UploadCompletedActivity`. The tool generates the activities as source code files that we can include in our project. The activities will have their `InterfaceType` and `EventName` or `MethodName` properties pre-populated, and include properties for all parameters in the communications. Run `wca.exe` with no parameters to see a list of options.

Fault Handling

Although fault handling is arguably a type of control flow, this section is dedicated to these activities so we can dive in with more detail. Fault handling in Windows Workflow handles exceptions that occur during execution. We can catch exceptions with fault handlers and perhaps try to recover from the error. We might try to compensate for a committed transaction, or send an alert to an administrative email address and wait for a missing file to reappear.

It is always a bad idea to blindly handle faults if we don't have a recovery plan. This is akin to *swallowing* exceptions in C# or Visual Basic. If the workflow throws an exception that we don't know how to handle, it is best to let the exception run its course and have the runtime terminate the workflow.

The FaultHandlersActivity

The FaultHandlers activity isn't an activity we can drag from the **Toolbox** into the workflow designer. Instead, the workflow designer will provide the activity for us when the condition is right. Many composite activities (like the WhileActivity, ListenActivity, SequenceActivity, TransactionScopeActivity, and others) can handle faults from their child activities using a **fault handlers view**.

We can view the FaultHandlers activity by right-clicking an activity and selecting **View Faults**. There is also a shortcut available to view fault handlers at the workflow level. The third tab from the left in the bottom of the workflow designer will take us to the fault handlers for the workflow (see the screenshot below). Inside this view we can use FaultHandler activities, discussed next.

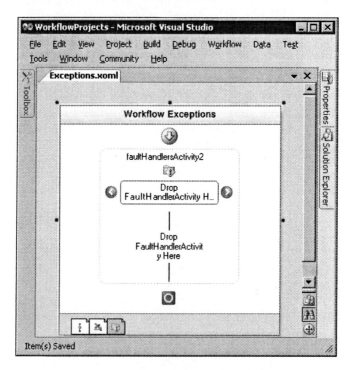

The FaultHandlerActivity

A `FaultHandler` activity is analogous to a catch statement in C# or Visual Basic. A `FaultHandler` can trap an exception and perform processing. When we are in the **Fault Handlers** view, we can drag a `FaultHandler` from the **Toolbox** into the area saying **Drop FaultHandlerActivity Here**. This area is the fault handlers **storyboard**. We can drop more than one `FaultHandler` into the storyboard, and click on handlers inside to select the handler we want to edit. Each handler has its own set of child activities that appear below the storyboard. We can drop activities in the area below the storyboard to perform different types of work for each fault handler. This is akin to the code inside a catch block.

The `FaultHandlerActivity` has a `FaultType` property. This property represents the type of exception we want to catch. If we set the `FaultType` property to the `System.Exception` type, we will handle all CLS-compliant exceptions. The handler will catch all exceptions of type `FaultType`, or any exception deriving from `FaultType`. The `Fault` property of this activity will let us bind the caught exception to a field or property.

The runtime will evaluate Fault Handlers in a left-to-right order. If the first Fault Handler has a `FaultType` of `System.Exception`, it will catch any exception and the runtime won't need to evaluate the other fault handlers. This is similar to how the multiple catch statements work in C# or Visual Basic — the catch blocks are evaluated in the order they appear until a match is found, and then no other catch statements are evaluated.

Transactions and Compensation

Traditional ACID (atomic, consistent, isolated, and durable) transactions are available in Windows Workflow. Under the covers, the runtime makes use of the `Transaction` class in the `System.Transactions` namespace. The `Transaction` class can manage transactions across different types of durable stores, including Microsoft SQL Server and other relational databases, and products like Microsoft Message Queuing. When needed, the `Transaction` class can use the Microsoft Distributed Transaction Coordinator (MSDTC) for heavy-weight two-phase commit transactions.

The TransactionScopeActivity

Like the `TransactionScope` class of `System.Transactions`, the `TransactionScope` activity will start a transaction and implicitly enlist any activities it contains into the transaction. The `TransactionOptions` property controls the timeout and the isolation level of the transaction.

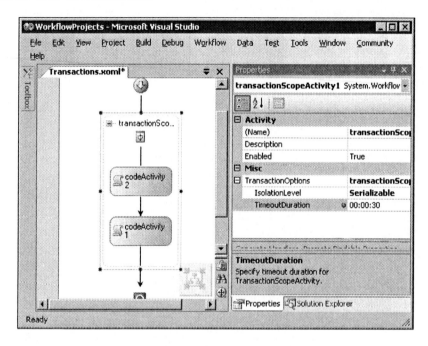

If the `TransactionScope` activity finishes with no errors it will automatically commit the transaction. If an exception occurs inside the scope but is not caught by a fault handler inside the scope, the activity will abort the transaction and roll back any work.

Compensation

In a long-running workflow, we can't leave a transaction open for hours, or days, or weeks at a time. A transaction will lock records and could prevent other queries from executing. Holding locks for long periods can kill scalability and bring applications to a grinding halt.

Instead of holding locks, we will typically commit transactions as soon as possible and move on with execution. If an error occurs at some later point, we counteract the previously completed transaction. We might not be able to *reverse* the transaction, but we might take other steps (cancel an order, credit an account) to counterbalance the transaction.

In WF, we can only formally compensate for activities that implement the `ICompensatableActivity` interface. The `CompensatableSequenceActivity` and the `CompensatableTransactionScopeActivity` are the two activities in the base class library that implement this interface.

The CompensatableSequenceActivity

A `CompensatableSequence` activity functions just like a `Sequence` activity with the addition of a compensation handler. We can view the compensation handler for this activity by right-clicking the activity and selecting **View Compensation Handler** (see the screenshot below).

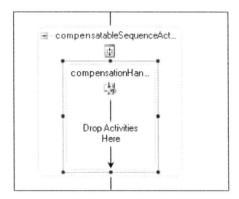

Inside of the compensation handler we can place activities to compensate for the activities that ran during the normal execution of the sequence. We will see how to trigger a compensation handler shortly.

The CompensatableTransactionScopeActivity

The `CompensatableTransactionScope` activity functions just like a `TransactionScope` activity but with the addition of a compensation handler. We can also view the compensation handler for this activity by right-clicking the activity and selecting **View Compensation Handler**. Inside the compensation handler we can use activities to define the logic that will compensate for the normal execution of the activity. Remember that compensation can only take place if a compensatable activity completes successfully.

The CompensateActivity

The Compensate activity starts the compensation of a previously completed and compensatable activity. We can only compensate for the activities that implement the ICompensatableActivity interface. We described the two compensatable activities provided by the base class library. We can also create our own custom activities that implement the ICompensatableActivity interface.

The Compensate activity's TargetActivityName property will direct the workflow to the ICompensatableActivity that needs compensated. The runtime will execute the target activity's compensation handler. A Compensate activity can only exist inside a fault handler or inside a compensation handler. When the activity is inside a compensation handler it can direct the compensation of nested transactions.

Conditions and Rules

Two activities in Windows Workflow thrive on conditions and rules. These activities are the Policy Activity and the Conditioned Activity Group (CAG). Although we could have listed the CAG as a control flow element, the CAG doesn't control the flow of execution as much as allow it to be controlled by conditions and rules.

The ConditionedActivityGroup

The CAG is a powerful activity that can use a combination of rules and code to reach a goal. The CAG conditionally executes activities until a condition evaluates to true. Inside of the CAG is a storyboard where we can drop activities for execution (see the screenshot on the next page). The CAG associates a WhenCondition with each activity in its storyboard, and the CAG will only execute an activity if the activity's WhenCondition evaluates to true. The CAG continues to re-evaluate the WhenCondition and re-execute the storyboard activities until its own UntilCondition evaluates to true.

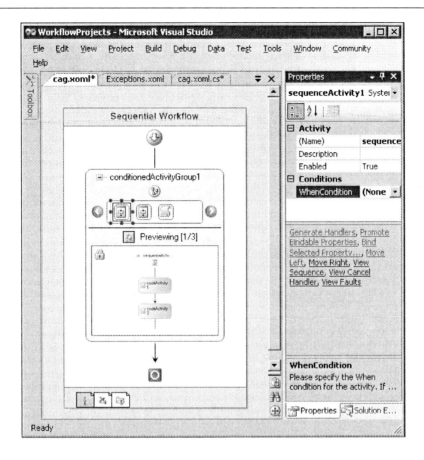

The WhenCondition and UntilCondition properties can use either declarative rules or code conditions. If we do not specify a WhenCondition for an activity, the activity will execute only once. If we do not specify an UntilCondition for the CAG, the CAG will continue to execute until all its activity's WhenCondition conditions return false.

We can click on each activity in the CAG's storyboard to set its WhenCondition, and also to preview or edit the activity in the bottom half of the CAG display. The small button in the middle of the CAG will toggle between preview and edit modes. In edit mode we can click on storyboard activities to set properties, or in the case of a composite activity like the Sequence activity, we can drag additional children inside.

The CAG will revaluate its UntilCondition each time a child activity completes. As soon as the condition returns true, the CAG will cancel any currently executing activities and close.

The PolicyActivity

The `Policy` activity is a rules engine that allows us to separate business logic from the workflow and declaratively define business policy. A **Rule Set** is a collection of rules for the `Policy` activity to execute, and each rule has conditions and actions. We can edit the rules using the WF **Rule Set Editor**, shown in the screenshot.

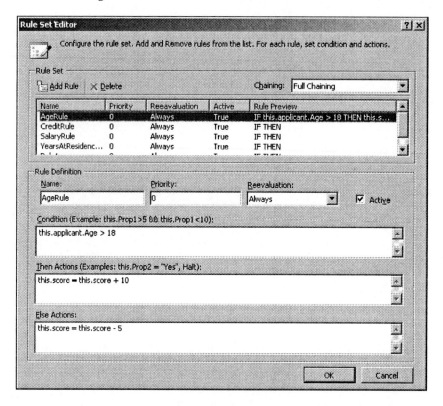

Notice each rule has a priority assigned. Rules with a higher priority will execute before rules with a lower priority. Rules with the same level priority execute in alphabetical order.

Each rule has an If-Then-Else format. We can assign actions to both the Then and Else results. A rule's actions can modify the fields and properties of a workflow, or the fields and properties of an object inside the workflow. Actions can also invoke methods.

By default, the `Policy` activity will execute the rule set using full forward chaining. If a rule changes the value of a field that some previous rule depended upon, the `Policy` activity will re-evaluate the previous rule. The `Policy` activity supports different forward chaining strategies, and each rule has a re-evaluation setting to control the number of times it can be re-evaluated. Chapter 9 will examine the `Policy` activity in great detail.

Web Services

No product would be complete today if it did not send or receive SOAP envelopes over HTTP. WF includes a number of activities that revolve around web services, both as a client and a server.

The InvokeWebServiceActivity

The `InvokeWebService` activity can call an external web service. When we drop the activity into the workflow designer, the familiar Visual Studio **Add Web Reference** dialog box will appear. This same dialog appears when we add a web reference to any type of .NET project in Visual Studio. We merely need to browse to a Web Service Definition Language (WSDL) document with the description of the web service. Visual Studio will retrieve the WSDL and generate a proxy class for the web service. We can then configure the activity with the method name to invoke, and bind parameters to fields or properties in our workflow (see the screenshot).

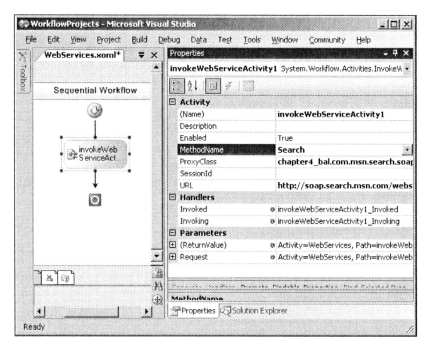

The `WebServiceActivity` includes `Invoking` and `Invoked` event handlers that fire before and after the web service call, respectively. We can use these events to pre- and post-process the parameters of the web service.

The WebServiceInputActivity

The `WebServiceInput` activity enables a workflow to receive a web service request. Just like the local communication activities we described earlier, this activity will first require us to define a contract (an interface). The activity will implement the interface. Once we've set the `InterfaceType` property, we can pick a method from the interface for the `MethodName` property, and then bind the incoming parameters to fields or properties.

Visual Studio 2005 allows us to right-click a workflow project and select **Publish As Web Service**. This command creates an ASP.NET project, complete with `.asmx` and `web.config` files, which will host our workflow as a web service.

The WebServiceOutputActivity

A `WebServiceOutput` activity pairs with a `WebServiceInput` activity to respond to a service request. We cannot use this activity without first configuring a `WebServiceInput` activity in our workflow. This activity has an `InputActivityName` property that will pair the activity with its input. The designer will then know the interface and method name we are implementing, and allow us to bind the `ReturnValue` property. The `ReturnValue` property is the web service response.

The WebServiceFaultActivity

The `WebServiceFault` activity allows us to raise an exception that the runtime will package into a SOAP exception. Like the output activity we just described, the `WebServiceFault` activity will pair with an input activity via the `InputActivityName` property. The `Fault` property will reference the exception we want to raise.

State Activities

All of the workflows we've examined so far have been sequential workflows. Windows Workflow also supports state-machine workflows, which is where the activities in this section come into play.

A state machine consists of a set of states. For instance, a state machine to model the workflow of a software bug might include the states open, assigned, closed, and deferred. The workflow must always be in one of these four states. State machines are completely event driven. Only when the workflow receives an event can the current state **transition** to a new state. A state machine must have an initial state, and optionally an ending state. When the state machine transitions to the ending state, the workflow is complete.

State machine workflows are a good fit for modeling a process where decisions come from *outside* the workflow. When we make a decision, like closing a bug, we have a local communication service raise an event to the workflow. The workflow keeps track of which state it is in, and which states it can transition into from the current state. For instance, we might say that an open bug has to be assigned before it can be closed, but it can move from the open state directly to the deferred state. The first step in setting up a state machine is defining the states.

The StateActivity

The `State` activity represents one of the states in a state machine. For our bug tracking workflow, we would have four `State` activities to drop into the designer — one each for open, closed, deferred, and assigned. Unlike a sequential workflow, we can place these activities anywhere on the design surface, because the state machine doesn't move from one activity to the next in any specific order. We will define the legal state transitions.

Every state machine workflow needs an **initial state**. We can set the initial state using the `InitialStateName` property of the workflow itself (see screenshot below). We can optionally set the `CompletedStateName` to a state that represents completion of the workflow. The state machine in the screenshot below has the four `State` activities for bug tracking: `OpenState`, `AssignedState`, `DeferredState`, and `ClosedState`.

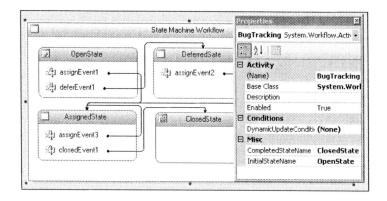

Inside each state, we can place the activities described below. Notice we can include a `State` activity inside a `State` activity. The recursive composition of states allows contained states to inherit the events and behavior of their containing state. Chapter 7 will cover these activities in more detail.

The StateInitializationActivity

The `StateInitialization` activity is a sequence activity that contains child activities. When the state machine transitions to a state, the children inside the initialization activity will execute. We can only have one initialization activity per state. Once we've dropped this activity inside a state, we can double-click to edit the children. In the screenshot below, we've added an initialize activity to `OpenState`, and can now add child activities of any type as children.

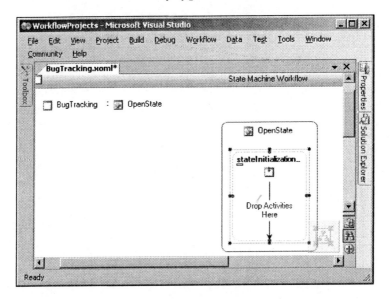

The StateFinalizationActivity

Like the initialize activity, the `StateFinalization` activity is a sequence activity with child activities inside. When the state machine transitions *out* of a state, the state's finalization activities will execute. There can be only one finalization activity inside each state.

The EventDrivenActivity

The `EventDriven` activity is also a sequence activity with children inside. The `EventDriven` activity, however, only executes when an event arrives. The first child activity must implement the `IEventActivity` interface, as the `HandleExternalEvent` activity does. You might remember we described this activity briefly when we discussed the `ListenActivity`.

A `State` activity can contain more than one `EventDriven` activity inside. For example, our `OpenState` state will have two `EventDriven` activities inside — one to handle a `BugAssigned` event, and one to handle a `BugDeferred` event. We do not allow the `OpenState` to handle a `BugClosed` event, because we don't want to transition from open to closed without going through the assigned state.

In the screenshot below, we've double-clicked on an `EventDriven` activity in `OpenState` to configure an event handler for the `BugAssigned` event. The event is part of a communication interface we've built with the `ExternalDataExchange` attribute, just as we did earlier in the section covering the `HandleExternalEvent` activity. The first activity in the `EventDriven` activity is, in fact, a `HandleExternalEvent` activity we've configured to handle the `BugAssigned` event. The last activity inside the sequence is a `SetState` activity, which we cover next.

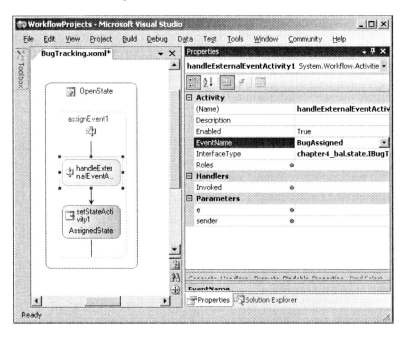

The SetStateActivity

The `SetState` activity transitions a state machine to a new state. In the screenshot below, we are handling the `BugAssigned` event. When a bug is assigned, we want to transition to the `AssignedState`, so we set the `TargetStateName` property to `AssignedState`. The `AssignedState` activity will then have its own set of `EventDriven` activities, each with `SetState` activities to transition to other states (and hopefully one day reach the `ClosedState`).

The workflow view of a state machine will examine the `SetState` activities inside and draw lines to represent state transitions. We can see in the screenshot below that state machine will only transition to the `ClosedState` activity from the `AssignedState` activity. We also see lines representing all the other state transitions.

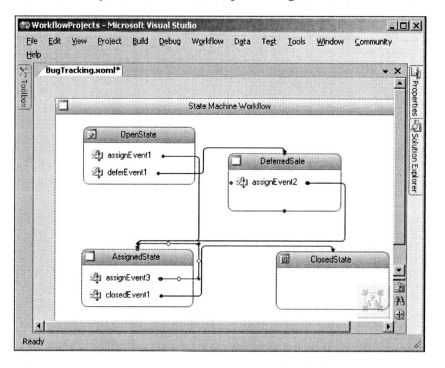

Summary

We've been through all of the activities in the Windows Workflow base activity library. We've seen event handling, local and remote communication, control flow, and more. As we outlined at the beginning, these activities are generic and general-purpose activities that can build powerful workflows and solve problems across a variety of business domains. However, WF allows us to build custom-tailored activities to solve our business problems, and this will be our next topic to cover.

5
Custom Activities

Building software with a general-purpose framework is fun, but not necessarily productive. Building software with a framework that specializes in solving our day-to-day problems can be fun and productive. We can tailor Windows Workflow to solve our day-to-day problems by writing custom activities. A custom activity might solve problems in a specific business domain such as a custom activity that can request tests on a patient's blood sample for healthcare applications. We could also write custom activities for a technology domain. If our applications make heavy use of Microsoft Message Queuing (MSMQ), it would make sense to build custom activities that interact with MSMQ.

We are going to start this chapter talking about why we would write custom activities, and then delve into different approaches for implementing custom activities. We will discuss how to build black box and white box activities using composition techniques. We will also look at using inheritance to build custom activities, and how to build validation and design-time behavior into our activities. Along the way, we will also discuss concepts central to building activities, like dependency properties and execution contexts. By the end of this chapter we should be able to evaluate the tradeoffs in using composition versus inheritance, and understand the techniques and technologies used to build custom activities.

Why Would I Build Custom Activities?

There are different motivations for building custom activities, so the answer to this question can depend on your perspective. Three possible motivations are:

- Building reusable components
- Extending Windows Workflow
- Building a domain-specific language

Reusability

We would never want the same five lines of code to appear twice in any application. Instead, we package reusable code into methods. In ASP.NET and Windows Forms applications, we would never want to drag-and-drop the same five controls into multiple forms. Instead, we write custom controls and reuse those controls in multiple forms. When change comes along (as it inevitably does), we can make a change in one place and see the change appear everywhere in an application, or even across multiple applications. We can reuse logic and code in Windows Workflow by building custom activities.

One way to build custom activities in Windows Workflow is through **activity composition**. We can *compose* custom activities out of smaller, more primitive activities—just as we compose custom UI controls out of smaller, more primitive UI controls. We can package these activities into activity libraries and reuse them in multiple workflows. Composition is about reuse.

Extensibility

The base activity library includes activities for control flow and executing workflows with certain semantics, but we are free to build custom activities with new control flow and execution semantics. There is nothing special about the activities inside the base activity library—they do not use a hidden API and the WF runtime doesn't treat Microsoft's activities any differently than it would treat our custom activities.

If a sequential workflow or state machine workflow doesn't fit our needs, we can devise our own execution style. If the `While` and `IfElse` activities are not flexible or expressive enough for our needs, we can write our own control flow activities, like a `ForEach` activity. Extensibility is about building new primitive activities.

Domain-Specific Languages

My doctor's financial software uses the terms *charges* and *receipts*. My bank's financial software uses the terms *debits* and *credits*. Even though both pieces of software manage the flow of money into and out of accounts, we would confuse the end users if we ever interchanged the two just because of their different vocabularies. One benefit of a Domain-Specific Language (DSL) is the ability to express solutions using the standard vocabulary of a problem domain.

However, a standard vocabulary is not the only advantage. A DSL allows us to work at a higher level of abstraction. Let's take an example of a document management application. One common task in document management solutions is the task of document approval. If a programmer is writing a document approval workflow, he or she will place and configure a `HandleExternalEvent` activity at the appropriate location to wait for the approval event. `HandleExternalEvent` is a general-purpose activity that can handle any type of event, and it requires knowledge of interfaces, types, and event handlers to set up properly.

On the other hand, our developer could implement a custom activity named `WaitForDocumentApproval`. In addition to using the native vocabulary of the document management domain, the custom activity would be pre-configured to handle the proper events. The activity shields the workflow designer from knowing about specific interfaces and types. The higher level of abstraction yields productivity benefits.

Now that we know a handful of motivations for *why* we would build a custom activity, let's look at *how* to build them.

How Do I Build Custom Activities?

There are two approaches to building a custom activity. One approach uses composition and the second approach uses derivation.

The composition approach is a similar experience to authoring a workflow. We use the designer to drag, drop, and configure activities inside a new custom activity, and then package the custom activity into an assembly for use in other workflow projects. The composition approach is a quick and easy path to reusable workflow components.

In the derivation approach, we derive a new activity from the `Activity` class. We can also derive from descendants of the `Activity` class to inherit more functionality. We can customize the design view, validation, serialization, and code-generation pieces of the activity. The derivation approach gives us the highest level of control and offers a path to extending Windows Workflow with custom code.

We will examine both of these approaches, but start with the composition approach.

Activity Composition

Let's return to the bug-tracking workflow we used in Chapter 4 to see if a custom activity can help us in building a bug-tracking application. The bug-tracking workflow is needed to request additional documentation for a bug. To request this documentation, the workflow communicates with a local service we built in Chapter 4 that implements the following interface:

```
[ExternalDataExchange]
interface IBugService
{
```

```
      bool RequestUpload(Guid id, string userName);
      event EventHandler<UploadCompletedEventArgs> UploadCompleted;
}
```

A workflow that needs documentation would first use a `CallExternalMethod` activity to invoke the `RequestUpload` method. Immediately afterwards, the workflow would use a `HandleExternalEvent` activity to wait for an `UploadCompleted` event. We need to insert and configure both of these activities into every workflow that might request an upload. Our goal is to replace these two activities with a single activity we customize for the job.

To get started, we'll build a workflow activity library. In the **New Project** dialog box of Visual Studio 2005, we select the **Workflow Activity Library** project type as shown in the screenshot below. The project type references all the WF assemblies that we'll need, and will build an assembly that we can reference from other workflow projects. We will give this project the name of `chapter5_activities`.

The activity library project will include a default activity (**Activity1.cs**). We can right-click and rename this activity to **GetUpload.cs**. This activity uses a **pure code** approach. In Chapter 2 we talked about using code only, XAML only, and a combination of XAML with code-behind. We have the same choices when building a custom activity. The XAML with code-behind and pure code approaches are available from the **New Item** dialog box in Visual Studio.

By default, the root activity in our custom activity is a `SequentialActivity`. In the design view, we can drag and drop activities from the **Toolbox** window inside the sequence. In the screenshot on the next page, we've placed a `CallExternalMethod` activity and a `HandleExternalEvent` activity inside. We've also configured these activities to invoke the `RequestUpload` method and handle the `UploadCompleted` events respectively. We won't configure any of the method and event parameters at this time.

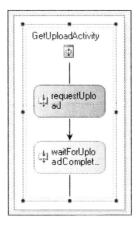

We can now compile our activity library project and produce an assembly. Next, we can create a new project to use this assembly. From the Visual Studio 2005 **File** menu, we can click **Add**, then **New Project**. We will select the **Sequential Workflow Console Application** as our project template and give the project the name of chapter5_workflows. To use the custom activity we just created, we'll right-click the new project and select **Add Reference**. In the **Projects** tab of the **Add Reference** dialog box, we can select our chapter_activities project.

When we are working with a workflow, Visual Studio will find custom activities in any assemblies we reference. The custom activities will appear in the **Toolbox** window when the workflow designer is open. We can see our GetUploadActivity activity in the following screenshot:

In the design view for our new sequential workflow, we can drop a GetUploadActivity inside the workflow (see the screenshot overleaf). Notice the activities inside our custom activity appear with padlock icons. We can't remove or add child activities inside custom activities built with composition (unless the activity is initially empty).

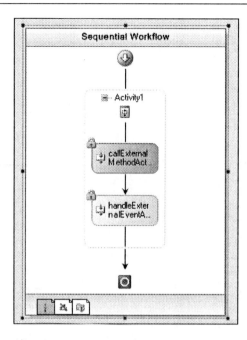

As it turns out, we can't even modify the *properties* of these activities inside the custom activity. A compiled composite activity becomes a **black box**. We cannot add, delete, or modify the child activities inside this black box. As custom activity designers, this black box behavior makes sense. We wouldn't want a workflow developer to change the `InterfaceType` or the `MethodName` properties of the `CallExternalMethod` activity. Changing these properties would break the intended functionality of our `GetUploadActivity`. Our custom activity needs to maintain its integrity.

For consumers of our custom activity, the black box presents a problem. Inside a workflow, we'll need to access the `id` and `userName` parameters of the `CallExternalMethod` activity to pass the correct data to the host. These properties are not accessible to the workflow, and the custom activity isn't usable.

As the authors of the custom activity, however, we can make some changes to make our component usable.

Opening a Black Box

Although a composite activity does not let the workflow designer get to properties and events inside the black box, we can *promote* properties from inside the black box and expose the properties to the outside world. **Property promotion** allows the author of a composite activity to decide which properties to hide from the outside world to maintain the integrity of the activity, and which properties to expose to the outside world to make the activity usable.

Property Promotion

Property promotion establishes a connection from a property on a parent activity to a property on one of the parent's child activities. You can think of property promotion as moving a property (or event) *up* the tree of activities to expose the property from the top level. We are going to return to our custom activity project and make the changes we need for the activity to be successful.

First, we need to decide what members we will promote. The CallExternalMethod activity has four candidates available for property promotion: the MethodInvoking handler, and the ReturnValue, id, and userName parameters. Of these four, let's choose to expose only the userName parameter. Exposing the userName property will allow the workflow to set a value for userName that the activity will pass to the host. The other three candidates are all implementation details we can keep hidden inside our composite activity. For instance, our custom activity can easily set the workflow instance ID parameter and inspect the ReturnValue without requiring assistance from the workflow itself. The userName parameter is the only value the composite activity will require from the workflow.

To promote the userName field, we need to open our custom activity in the designer and right-click on the CallExternalMethod activity to open the **Properties** window. In the **Properties** window, we click in the text box next to the userName field and then click the ellipsis button that will appear on the right-hand side of the text box. The button click will open the binding dialog box shown in the following screenshot:

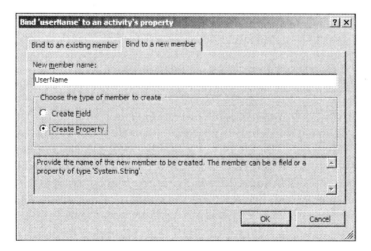

Property promotion adds a new property to our custom activity. The property will have the name UserName. Once we click **OK**, the designer will take care of a couple of tasks for us. First, the designer will generate the code for a **dependency property** in our custom activity. Just so we know — the designer is not performing any magic.

We could perform property promotion by hand. Let's look at the code the designer generates in our custom activity's code-behind file:

```
public static DependencyProperty UserNameProperty =
    DependencyProperty.Register(
            "UserName",
            typeof(System.String),
            typeof(chapter5_activities.GetUploadActivity));

[DesignerSerializationVisibilityAttribute(
    DesignerSerializationVisibility.Visible)]
[BrowsableAttribute(true)]
[CategoryAttribute("Parameters")]
public String UserName
{
    get
    {
        return ((string)(base.GetValue(
            GetUploadActivity.UserNameProperty)));
    }
    set
    {
        base.SetValue(
            GetUploadActivity.UserNameProperty, value);
    }
}
```

The dependency property has some metadata associated via attributes, such as the BrowsableAttribute. This particular piece of metadata tells the workflow designer to let a user see the property in the **Properties** window. We are going to return to dependency properties later in the chapter to examine this code in more detail.

The designer's second job was to connect the userName parameter of our CallExternalMethod activity to this new UserName dependency property on the parent activity. When we close the binding dialog, we'll see the userName property looks like what we see in screenshot on the next page. This is the **activity binding** syntax in WF. The activity binding tells the runtime to look at the UserName property of the GetUploadActivity when fetching the value for this parameter. There is now a connection between this userName parameter and the UserName dependency property on our activity. We will return to discuss more details of activity binding in just a bit.

Notice at the bottom of the **Properties** window shown in screenshot opposite, there is a **Promote Bindable Properties** command. This command will generate dependency properties and bindings for *all* of the parameters and handlers in the activity—in our case we chose to expose only userName.

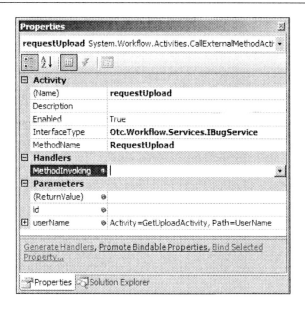

Now the workflow can set the `UserName` property of our activity, and the value will pass (bind) into this `userName` parameter for the `CallExternalMethod` activity. Now we need to return to some of the *implementation details* we discussed earlier. Specifically, for our activity to work, we will also need to pass an `id` parameter to the external method. This parameter is the instance ID of the executing workflow. We did not promote this parameter, so it is invisible to the outside world and we will need to manage it ourselves. Let's add the following code to our custom activity's code file:

```
private void requestUpload_MethodInvoking(object sender,
                                          EventArgs e)
{
    uploadID = this.WorkflowInstanceId;
}

Guid uploadID = Guid.Empty;
```

This code creates a private field named `uploadID`. The `uploadID` field will hold the workflow instance ID. We set this field in a method named `requestUpload_ MethodInvoking`. We plan to call this method just before the `CallExternalMethod` activity calls into the host process.

For this to work, we need to establish some more bindings in the **Property** window for the `CallExternalMethod` activity. In the figure overleaf, we've set the `CallExternalMethod` activity's `MethodInvoking` property to the `requestUpload_ MethodInvoking` method we just built in our code file. Our method will now fire just before the activity invokes the external method. We've also bound the activity's `id` parameter to the `uploadID` field in our class.

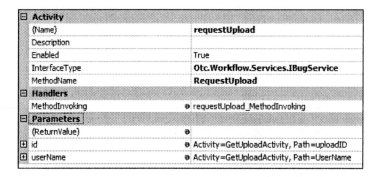

Activity	
(Name)	**requestUpload**
Description	
Enabled	True
InterfaceType	**Otc.Workflow.Services.IBugService**
MethodName	**RequestUpload**
Handlers	
MethodInvoking	requestUpload_MethodInvoking
Parameters	
(ReturnValue)	
id	Activity=GetUploadActivity, Path=uploadID
userName	Activity=GetUploadActivity, Path=UserName

The next step for our custom activity might be to promote properties from the `HandleExternalEvent` activity. For instance, if the workflow depends on the filename that is part of the incoming event arguments, we'd need a dependency property on our custom activity to expose the filename. We could promote the entire event argument (`e`), or create a dependency property from scratch and expose only the filename portion of the event arguments.

Composition Summary

We've created a reusable chunk of workflow with a custom activity. We can drop this activity inside any workflow instead of dropping and configuring the underlying custom activities. We've promoted properties inside the activity for the workflow author to use. The properties allow the workflow author to parameterize the activity for a specific job. The following screenshot shows how our custom activity appears in a new workflow (complete with the new `UserName` property).

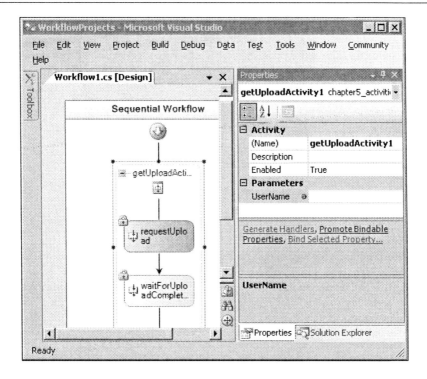

Before we jump into the second approach for building custom activities, we need to revisit the subject of dependency properties and activity binding. Dependency properties and activity binding are both important and related pieces of infrastructure for building custom activities and workflows in general.

Dependency Properties

The ultimate goal of a dependency property is to manage *state*. The dependency property is not unique to Windows Workflow; it is also present in WF's XAML sibling—Windows Presentation Foundation. A dependency property enables a handful of critical features in WF:

- Activity property binding
- Attached properties
- Meta-properties

Every class that uses a dependency property will ultimately derive from the abstract `DependencyObject` class. Shown in the screenshot overleaf, the `DependencyObject` provides methods to manipulate dependency properties, like `GetValue` and `SetValue`. Also shown in the following figure is the `DependencyProperty` class.

This class represents the metadata that describes a dependency property, like the **Name** and **OwnerType**.

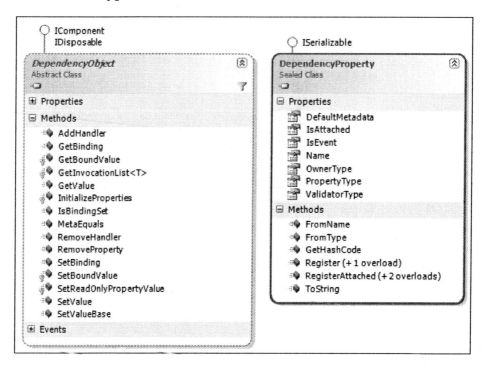

We've already seen some of these DependencyObject methods used when we created a UserName property for our custom composite activity. Let's look again at a portion of that code that the designer generated:

```
public String UserName
{
    get
    {
        return ((string)(base.GetValue(
            GetUploadActivity.UserNameProperty)));
    }
    set
    {
        base.SetValue(
            GetUploadActivity.UserNameProperty, value);
    }
}
```

Our `UserName` property does not have a backing private field as many properties will have. Instead, the property retrieves and sets values using the `GetValue` and `SetValue` methods from the base class. Our activity has these methods available because it ultimately derives from the `DependencyObject` class.

We never manipulate dependency properties directly; we only touch them through these special `GetValue` and `SetValue` methods. You can think of the `DependencyObject` as a gateway between property state and our code. By putting itself in the middle, the `DependencyObject` can perform a great deal of magic, including data binding, change notifications, and more.

Internally, a `DependencyObject` maintains a generic `Dictionary` of dependency properties and their values. Remember the `DependencyProperty` class in the screenshot on the previous page? An instance of this class will function as a key into the dependency property dictionary. What follows is the rest of the code that the designer generated for our `UserName` property.

```
public static DependencyProperty UserNameProperty =
    DependencyProperty.Register(
            "UserName",                   // name
            typeof(System.String),        // type
            typeof(GetUploadActivity)); // owner
```

When our `UserName` property calls `base.GetValue` or `base.SetValue`, it passes along this `DependencyObject` named `UserNameProperty`. This is the key into the object's dictionary of dependency properties. The key provides the name of the dependency property, as well as its type and the type of its owner.

Before we decide on when to use dependency properties versus when to use regular properties, let's look at the features dependency properties facilitate: activity binding, attached properties, and meta-properties.

Activity Binding

There are certainly times when we won't be able to set the value of a property at design time. The values for some properties will only be known at run time. For instance, we know what type of interface our composite activity's `CallExternalMethod` activity will be working with, so we set the `InterfaceType` property of this activity at design time. We *don't* know what value to use for the `userName` parameter at design time, because this value won't be available until the workflow is up and running for a specific user.

What we did for the `userName` parameter was to *bind* the parameter to a `UserName` property on our composite activity. The **Properties** window for `userName` back in the screenshot displaying the **Property** window for the `CallExternalMethod` activity in the section *Property Promotion* contained the following: **Activity=GetUploadActivity, Path=UserName**. When we call `GetValue` for the `userName` parameter, the dependency property system will go to the `GetUploadActivity` activity and fetch the value of the `UserName` property.

Activity binding is a powerful mechanism we can use to wire together run time data with activity properties. This is similar to how data binding in .NET wires together data from a data source with user interface elements in a Windows form or web form. A common use of activity binding is to bind the output parameter of one activity to an input parameter of a later activity. This technique means we don't have the burden of shuffling data from one activity to the next.

Binding actually takes place with the `ActivityBind` class. The class has a `Name` and a `Path` property that allow the `SetValue` and `GetValue` methods to find the activity and activity member to bind against. The code generated by the workflow designer for the `userName` binding we created earlier would look like the following:

```
ActivityBind activitybind1 = new ActivityBind();
activitybind1.Name = "GetUploadActivity";
activitybind1.Path = "UserName";
```

We can pass this `ActivityBind` object to the `SetBinding` method of a `DependencyObject`. The `SetBinding` method looks just like the `SetValue` method, except we pass binding information instead of an actual value of a property. Activity binding is also available in XAML. The binding syntax uses curly brackets, as seen in the following code snippet:

```
<ns0:GetUploadActivity
        x:Name="getUploadActivity1"
        UserName="{ActivityBind Workflow1,Path=userName}" />
```

Theoretically, we could implement the same binding behavior using normal properties in C# or Visual Basic. We'd have to write all of the plumbing in the property `get` and `set` methods to make the binding magic work. Dependency properties do all of the hard work for us.

Attached Properties

We can *attach* a dependency property to any other object derived from `DependencyObject`. This means we can extend any activity in Windows Workflow with additional, custom properties at run time.

One scenario where attached properties are commonly used is when a parent activity needs to append information to each of its child activities. A concrete example is the `ConditionedActivityGroup`. The CAG, if you remember from Chapter 4, conditionally executes one or more child activities based on a `When` condition that is associated with each child. In the workflow designer, every child activity in a CAG *appears* to have its own `When` property, but this is an illusion created by the magic of dependency properties. It would be silly to give every activity a `When` property just so it could work inside a CAG.

Let's say we have a `CodeActivity` inside a CAG, and we've written a `CodeCondition` method named `MyCondition`. In the designer, we will set the `When` property of the activity to `MyCondition`, and the designer will generate code equivalent to the following:

```
CodeCondition codecondition1 = new CodeCondition();

codecondition1.Condition +=
  new System.EventHandler<ConditionalEventArgs>(MyCondition);

codeActivity1.SetValue(
    ConditionedActivityGroup.WhenConditionProperty,
    codecondition1);
```

The call to `SetValue` will place the CAG's `When` property *inside* the `CodeActivity`'s dictionary of property values. Then `When` property is now *attached* to the `CodeActivity`. Of course, XAML has a notation for attached properties too, which we can see below:

```
<ConditionedActivityGroup x:Name="conditionedActivityGroup1">
  <CodeActivity x:Name="codeActivity1"
        ExecuteCode="codeActivity1_ExecuteCode">
    <ConditionedActivityGroup.WhenCondition>
      <CodeCondition Condition="MyCondition" />
    </ConditionedActivityGroup.WhenCondition>
  </CodeActivity>
</ConditionedActivityGroup>
```

When an activity wants to have a property that it will attach to other activities, it can register the dependency property with the `RegisterAttached` method of `DependencyProperty` instead of the `Register` method.

Meta-Properties

There are two types of dependency properties. There are meta-based properties and instance-based properties. The value of a meta-based property must be set at design time and can never change during run time. This means we cannot bind a meta-property, since binding would set a value at run time. Instance-based properties can be set at design time or at run time, and take advantage of activity binding.

Meta-based properties are a safety net to ensure the integrity of an activity. For instance, when we configured our `CallExternalEvent` activity earlier, we set `InterfaceType` and `MethodName` properties. Based upon those two settings, the designer makes other properties available for us to configure (the parameters of the external method). Given the parameter configuration, it would be dangerous to change the `InterfaceType` or `MethodName` properties at run time. All other configurations would break. Thus, the `CallExternalEvent` activity defines these two properties as meta-based dependency properties and they are immutable at run time.

When we call the `Register` method to enter a dependency property into the `DependencyProperty` type catalog, we can pass an optional `PropertyMetaData` object as a parameter. The constructor of this object can take a `DependencyPropertyOptions` enumeration to specify if a property is a meta-property. The following code registers a meta-property by the name of `InterfaceType`:

```
public static DependencyProperty InterfaceTypeProperty =
    DependencyProperty.Register(
            "InterfaceType",
            typeof(Type),
            typeof(GetUploadActivity),
            new PropertyMetadata(DependencyPropertyOptions.Metadata)
    );
```

Dependency Property Summary

An obvious question at this point is: when do we use a plain property and when do we use a dependency property? The short answer is: when we want to define a meta-property, attach the property, or allow intra-activity binding on the property, we need a dependency property. All three features are significant to custom activity development. With this in mind, let's continue to look at building custom activities with the derivation model.

Derivation

Technically, there isn't an enormous difference between the composition and derivation approaches for building custom activities. When we built our `GetUploadActivity` earlier, the new activity did derive from the `SequenceActivity` class. Composition and derivation both use inheritance. Many of the topics we'll cover in this section we could also apply to `GetUploadActivity`.

Derivation versus composition is more a *state of mind*. In composition, we focus on arranging child activities inside a custom activity, and we build bigger activities from smaller activities. With derivation, we focus on designing a single activity—its properties and execution model. The derivation approach is often the low-level approach. Let's build a custom activity with derivation that writes to the console.

ConsoleWriteActivity

For this activity, we will start with a simple class file. No XAML, no designers, just the following C# code:

```csharp
using System;
using System.Workflow.ComponentModel;
using System.ComponentModel;
using System.Workflow.ComponentModel.Design;

namespace OdeToCode.WF.CustomActivities
{
    public class ConsoleWriteActivity : Activity
    {
        public string Text
        {
            get { return _text; }
            set { _text = value; }
        }
        private string _text;

        protected override ActivityExecutionStatus Execute(
            ActivityExecutionContext executionContext)
        {
            Console.WriteLine(Text);
            return ActivityExecutionStatus.Closed;
        }
    }
}
```

We've derived our activity from the `System.Workflow.ComponentModel.Activity` class. `Activity` is the foundation for all activities in WF. Our activity has a simple `Text` property. We did not make this a dependency property yet, so the property won't be able to participate in data binding. We'll still be able to set the property to a string literal in the workflow designer.

The most important feature of the class is the `Execute` method. By overriding the `Execute` method, we've taken full responsibility for the behavior of this activity. When the time comes for our activity to run, the runtime will invoke our `Execute` method and we will write the `Text` property to the console. We then have to inform the runtime that our activity has finished executing by returning an execution status result of `Closed`.

At this point, we can compile the custom activity. If we then create a new workflow and open the workflow designer, this new activity should appear in the **Toolbox** (of course, we need a reference to the assembly containing the activity). If we drag the new activity from the **Toolbox** and drop it into a workflow, the activity will look similar to activities from the base class library (see the screenshot below).

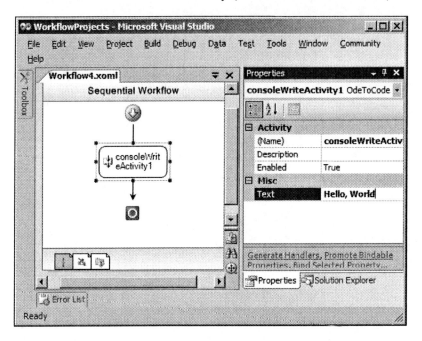

Notice the `Text` property of our activity is available in the **Properties** window (although the property appears in a category named **Misc**). We can control design-time features of our properties with attributes in the `System.ComponentModel` and `System.Workflow.ComponentModel` namespaces. For instance, adding the highlighted code to our `Text` property provides a default value, a description, and a category for the property.

```
[DefaultValue("")]
[Description("The text to write to the console")]
[Category("Activity")]
public string Text
{
    get { return _text; }
    set { _text = value; }
}
```

Attributes are not just for our properties. We can control our activity's behavior and appearance with attributes, too.

Activity Components

We can associate *activity components* with our activity to tweak its behavior. Two important component types are **activity designers** and **activity validators**. We associate components with an activity using attributes. Obviously, these components are optional since we have a working custom activity that did not use any components. Nevertheless, most non-trivial custom activities will use these components to enhance the designer experience.

What happens if a workflow author never assigns a value to the Text property of our custom activity? Our ConsoleWrite activity would not be useful without a valid Text property, so we'd have to assume the author is making a mistake. If we associate a validator with our activity, we could give the author feedback about the problem.

Activity Validators

Activity validators execute during design and compilation to ensure our activity has the proper configuration for execution at run time. To perform validation we need to derive a new class from the ActivityValidator class and override the Validate method. The following Validate method will make sure our custom control has a non-empty Text property:

```
public override ValidationErrorCollection Validate(
    ValidationManager manager, object obj)
{
    ValidationErrorCollection errors = base.Validate(manager, obj);

    ConsoleWriteActivity activity = obj as ConsoleWriteActivity;

    if (activity.Parent != null &&
       String.IsNullOrEmpty(activity.Text))
    {
       errors.Add(
            ValidationError.GetNotSetValidationError("Text"));
    }

    return errors;
}
```

We add all validation errors to a ValidationErrorCollection and return the collection to the caller. Notice we check to see if the activity has a parent activity. This is because the Validate method will execute when we are compiling the custom activity itself. During that time, the activity will have a null Text property. If the activity has a parent, then we can assume the activity is inside of a workflow and needs validation.

We attach the validator to our custom activity using an `ActivityValidator` attribute.

```
[ActivityValidator(typeof(ConsoleWriteValidator))]
public class ConsoleWriteActivity : Activity
{
    // ...
}
```

Activity validators are not limited to checking properties—we could check anything. For instance, we might decide that our custom activity should only appear as the child activity of a `While` activity. We could check the parent property's type and raise a validation error if the type is not a `While` activity.

Activity Designers

Activity designers control the appearance and behavior of an activity at design time. We can derive a class from `ActivityDesigner` and override its virtual methods. By overriding the `OnPaint` method, we can draw our activity's shape on the designer surface. We can also override many of the methods familiar to Windows UI developers—`OnMouseDown`, `OnDragOver`, and more. The following code implements a designer for our custom activity:

```
public class ConsoleWriteDesigner : ActivityDesigner
{
    ConsoleWriteActivity _activity;

    protected override void Initialize(Activity activity)
    {
        _activity = activity as ConsoleWriteActivity;
        base.Initialize(activity);
    }

    protected override Size OnLayoutSize(
                ActivityDesignerLayoutEventArgs e)
    {
        return new Size(120, 70);
    }

    protected override void OnPaint(
                ActivityDesignerPaintEventArgs e)
    {
        e.Graphics.FillRectangle(Brushes.Black,
                            Location.X, Location.Y,
                            Size.Width, Size.Height);

        StringFormat format = new StringFormat();
```

```
format.Alignment = StringAlignment.Center;
Rectangle rect = new Rectangle(Location.X, Location.Y,
                                Size.Width, 15);
e.Graphics.DrawString(Activity.QualifiedName,
                    DesignerTheme.Font,
                    Brushes.Yellow, rect, format);

using(Font font = new Font("Lucida Console", 7))
{
    e.Graphics.DrawString("> " + _activity.Text, font,
                        Brushes.White, rect.X, rect.Y + 20);
}
        }
    }
}
```

The Initialize method gives us an opportunity to obtain a reference to our activity. The OnLayoutSize method lets us tell the designer how much space our activity will take on the drawing surface. In the OnPaint method we try to simulate the look of a small console window. We'll draw a black background and write out the activity's Text property in a white font. The result is in the screenshot below:

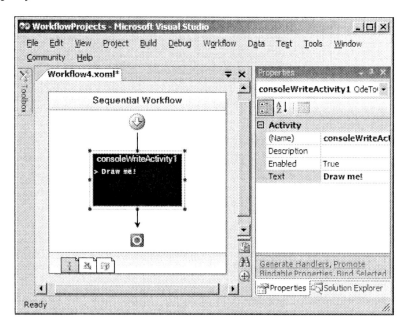

Of course, before the designer will work we need to associate our custom activity with the designer.

```
[ActivityValidator(typeof(ConsoleWriteValidator))]
[Designer(typeof(ConsoleWriteDesigner))]
public class ConsoleWriteActivity : Activity
{
    // ...
}
```

The custom activity we've built in this section is relatively simple. If we want to build advanced custom activities, we'll need to learn more about the ActivityExecutionContext class we saw earlier in our activity's Execute method. We also need to learn more about the life cycle of activities.

Activity Execution

Every activity in Windows Workflow must be in one of six states. These states are represented by the ActivityExecutionStatus enumeration: Initialized, Executing, Closed, Canceling, Compensating, and Faulting. All activities begin in the Initialized state, and all activities end in the Closed state. The possible state transitions are shown in the figure below:

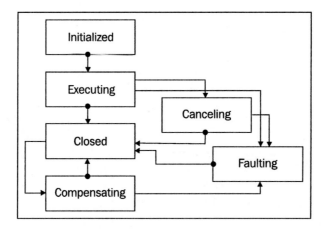

There are a couple of important comments to make about this diagram. First, the only way for an activity to transition to the Closed state is for the activity to announce to the workflow runtime that it is finished executing. An activity makes this announcement by returning ActivityExecutionStatus.Closed from one of the virtual methods discussed in the next paragraph.

All other state transitions coincide with a virtual method call to an activity. For example, the runtime invokes an activity's Execute method when the activity reaches the Executing state. The runtime invokes the Cancel method when the activity reaches the Canceling state. The methods and their associated state are listed in the table below:

Method	State
Initialize	Initialized
Execute	Executing
Cancel	Canceling
HandleFault	Faulting
Compensate	Compensating

The Execute, Cancel, HandleFault, and Compensate methods all return ActivityExecutionStatus as a result. Returning ActivityExecutionStatus. Closed from any of these methods will transition the activity to the Closed state. It is not possible to make other transitions using the return value of these methods. For instance, returning ActivityExecutionStatus.Canceling from the Execute method will not move the activity to the Canceling state—the WF runtime would throw an exception. An activity can only hold its current state, or announce it is complete. The WF runtime arranges all other transitions.

Another important observation about the state diagram in the screenshot on the previous page is that once an activity reaches the Closed state, it can *never* go back to the Executing state. Windows Workflow treats each activity as a unit of work. When an activity closes, it is complete. If transactions are involved, the runtime may decide to reverse the unit of work by moving the activity to the Compensating state, but the activity may never again initialize or execute. This fact has implications for composite activities that manage the execution of child activities. Let's turn our attention from execution status to execution context.

Execution Context

Let's take a quick look at the Execute method of our custom activity again:

```
protected override ActivityExecutionStatus Execute(
    ActivityExecutionContext executionContext)
{
    Console.WriteLine(Text);
    return ActivityExecutionStatus.Closed;
}
```

We see the Execute method returns an ActivityExecutionStatus of Closed to tell the workflow runtime it is complete. But what is this incoming parameter of type ActivityExecutionContext? An ActivityExecutionContext (AEC) represents the execution environment of an activity. The AEC object is a gateway to the services inside the WF runtime (it provides a generic `GetService` method), and provides methods for scheduling the execution of activities (`ExecuteActivity`, `CloseActivity`, `CancelActivity`). The AEC is shown in the class diagram below:

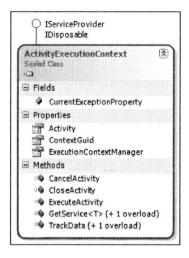

Understanding how to use the AEC is important if we have child activities to manage.

Custom Composite Activities

When we override the `Execute` method, we become responsible for managing the execution of our child activities. We have to manage this execution by coordinating with the WF runtime, and this coordination takes place using the AEC. We would never want to call the `Execute` method of a child activity directly because the Windows Workflow runtime will not be aware of what is happening with the activity. Instead of calling `Execute` directly, we schedule execution of a child activity using the AEC's `ExecuteActivity` method.

The WF runtime then works with the AEC to schedule activity execution and enforce rules. For instance, the runtime would not let us use `ExecuteActivity` to run an activity that is already in the `Closed` state. Such an operation would violate the legal state transitions for an activity and results in an exception.

If we were deriving a custom activity from the `CompositeActivity` class, our `Execute` method would follow the pattern in the code below:

```
protected override ActivityExecutionStatus Execute(
    ActivityExecutionContext executionContext)
{
    _currentIndex = 0;
```

```
Activity child = EnabledActivities[0];
child.Closed +=
    new EventHandler<ActivityExecutionStatusChangedEventArgs>
        (child_Closed);
executionContext.ExecuteActivity(child);
return ActivityExecutionStatus.Executing;
```

```
}
```

Here we are looking at our child activities through the EnabledActivities collection provided by our base class. We pull the first child activity from the collection and wire up an event handler for its Closed event. We then ask the WF runtime to schedule the activity for execution with the ExecuteActivity method. We need to return a status of Executing at this point, because we need to wait for all of the child activities to execute before we close our activity. Returning a status of Executing is common for activities that need to wait on an event. In this case we will be waiting for our first child activity to close, but we could also be waiting for a message to arrive in a queue.

When the child fires its Closed event, we need to continue the above pattern by fetching the next child activity (if any), subscribing to the Closed event, and scheduling the child for execution.

```
void child_Closed(object sender,
                ActivityExecutionStatusChangedEventArgs e)
{
    ActivityExecutionContext context = sender
                            as ActivityExecutionContext;
    e.Activity.Closed -= child_Closed;
    _currentIndex++;

    if (_currentIndex < EnabledActivities.Count)
    {
        Activity child = EnabledActivities[_currentIndex];
        child.Closed +=
            new EventHandler<ActivityExecutionStatusChangedEventArgs>
                (child_Closed);
        context.ExecuteActivity(child);
    }
    else
    {
        context.CloseActivity();
    }
}
```

Before we look for the next child to run, we unsubscribe from the Closed event of the child that just finished. If we have no enabled activities left to run, we can announce to the runtime that we have completed execution by invoking the AEC's CloseActivity event.

The above code moves sequentially through a collection of child activities — this is similar to how a SequenceActivity would behave. If instead we are writing a custom activity to loop over an activity multiple times, we need to use a different approach. Remember, each activity only reaches the Executing state *once*. If we need to execute an activity more than once we need to create a new execution context.

If we think of how the While activity executes, we are tempted to think the While activity executes the same activity multiple times. In reality, the While activity spawns a new ActivityExecutionContext each time it executes its child activity. Spawning an AEC creates a clone of the child activity. The original child activity will be known as the **template activity**, and each iteration of the while loop will create a copy of the template. This process is visualized in the screenshot below:

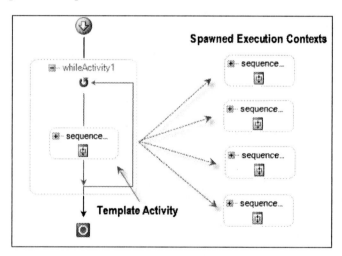

The essence of the While activity would follow the pattern in the code below:

```
ActivityExecutionContextManager manager;
manager = executionContext.ExecutionContextManager;

ActivityExecutionContext newContext;
newContext = manager.CreateExecutionContext(EnabledActivities[0]);
newContext.Activity.Closed +=
    new EventHandler<ActivityExecutionStatusChangedEventArgs>
        (Activity_Closed);
newContext.ExecuteActivity(newContext.Activity);
```

Given the context the runtime passes to the activity, we pull out the context manager and create a new context for our child activity with the `CreateExecutionContext` method. Using this new context we subscribe to the `Closed` event, and schedule the child to run. The `CreateExecutionContext` method will clone the activity we pass as a parameter. This is a deep clone, so if `EnabledActivities[0]` is itself a composite activity, the method will clone the composite activity and all of the composite activity's children.

Windows Workflow uses spawned execution contents to manage compensation. Each activity represents exactly one unit of work. If the activity inside the `While` activity needs to perform compensation, it does so by forcing each cloned activity to compensate its particular unit of work. If the `While` activity behaved differently and executed the same activity repeatedly, these units of work would be lost, and compensation would be impossible. Remember to use this pattern with `CreateExecutionContext` when creating a custom control with a looping control flow.

Summary

In this chapter we've looked at two techniques for building custom activities in Windows Workflow. Using composition, we can quickly build a reusable piece of workflow logic. Although a custom activity becomes a black box inside, we can expose the details a workflow author would need to configure our component using dependency properties and activity binding.

Derivation was a second approach to building a custom activity. With derivation, we override the Execute method of an activity and take complete control of its execution logic. Derivation allows us to build new forms of control flow and new execution semantics. With all custom activities we can add activity components to perform validation and provide custom designer behavior. We associate activity components with an activity using attributes.

6

Workflow Hosting

Windows Workflow is a runtime and not an application. A host process must load and launch the workflow runtime before starting a workflow. The host process tells the runtime the types of workflows to create, and the runtime manages the life cycle of the workflows and notifies the host process about important life cycle events, such as workflow completion and termination. The runtime isn't particular about the type of host it lives inside. The host process could be a smart client application running on an office desktop machine, or an ASP.NET worker process running on a server in the rack of a data center. All the host processes needs is the ability to load the .NET 3.0 Workflow assemblies.

A host can also customize the workflow runtime by layering additional **services** on top of the runtime's base feature set. These services can provide persistence support for long-running workflows, tracking support for monitoring workflow execution, and more. Recall the `ExternalDataExchangeService` we've used in previous chapters. We added this service to the runtime when we needed communication between a workflow and its host process. Not all applications will require this feature, so the service is an optional component we add as needed.

In this chapter, we are going to take a closer look at the Windows Workflow runtime and its available services. We'll start with the logging, tracing, and configuration options available for the workflow runtime. Next, we'll look at the scheduling services, which provide threads for the runtime to execute workflows. We will also examine persistence services, which allow us to save workflow state information to a durable store. Finally, we'll cover tracking services that allow us to monitor workflow execution.

The Workflow Runtime

We've used the runtime in previous chapters, but let's review what we've learned so far. The `WorkflowRuntime` class is the host's gateway to Windows Workflow. A host creates an instance of the class, and then subscribes to one or more of the events mentioned in the table below. These events report state changes for all workflow instances that the runtime is executing.

Name	Occurs
WorkflowAborted	When an instance aborts
WorkflowCompleted	When the instance completes
WorkflowCreated	When a successful call to CreateWorkflow completes
WorkflowIdled	When a workflow enters an idle state
WorkflowLoaded	When a persistence service restores a workflow instance
WorkflowPersisted	When a persistence service saves a workflow
WorkflowResumed	When workflow execution continues after a suspension
WorkflowStarted	When a workflow firsts starts execution

The code required to create the runtime and subscribe to events is relatively straightforward. The following example creates the runtime, subscribes to the `WorkflowCompleted` and `WorkflowTerminated` events, and then runs a new workflow instance.

```
using(WorkflowRuntime runtime = new WorkflowRuntime())
using(AutoResetEvent reset = new AutoResetEvent(false))
{
    runtime.WorkflowCompleted += delegate { reset.Set(); };
    runtime.WorkflowTerminated += delegate { reset.Set(); };
    runtime.StartRuntime();

    WorkflowInstance instance;
    instance = runtime.CreateWorkflow(typeof(SimpleWorkflow));
    instance.Start();
    reset.WaitOne();
}
```

The `WorkflowRuntime` class provides public methods like the `CreateWorkflow` and `StartRuntime` methods seen above, to manage the environment and the workflows. These methods can start and stop the runtime, create and retrieve workflows, and add and remove services inside the runtime. We'll be exploring some of these methods in more detail later.

Typically, we wouldn't create a runtime just to execute a single workflow. Most applications will keep the runtime around for the life of the process and run multiple workflows. However, we want to use this simple bit of code to demonstrate configuration and logging features of the WF runtime.

Workflow Runtime Logging

The .NET Framework provides a tracing API in the `System.Diagnostics` namespace. Windows Workflow uses this tracing API to log information about what is happening inside the runtime. Trace information is far more detailed than the information provided by the public events of the `WorkflowRuntime` class. To get to the trace information we first need to enable one or more **trace sources** in the workflow runtime.

When to Use Tracing

Tracing isn't used during normal operation of an application as it can create performance bottlenecks. However, tracing can be invaluable when tracking down performance problems or the cause of an exception. We can't use a debugger to step into the code of the WF runtime, but we can enable logging to see what is happening inside.

There are five trace sources available in WF. Each trace source supplies diagnostic information from a different functional area of Windows Workflow. We can enable these sources in code, or inside the application's configuration file. The following configuration file will configure all five trace sources:

```
<?xml version="1.0" encoding="utf-8" ?>
<configuration>
  <system.diagnostics>
    <switches>

        <add name="System.Workflow.Runtime" value="All" />
        <add name="System.Workflow.Runtime.Hosting" value="All" />
        <add name="System.Workflow.Runtime.Tracking"
                                            value="Critical" />
        <add name="System.Workflow.Activities" value="Warning" />
        <add name="System.Workflow.Activities.Rules" value="Off" />
        <add name="System.Workflow LogToFile" value="1" />

    </switches>
  </system.diagnostics>
</configuration>
```

Inside the `<switches>` section we see the name of each trace source. Each source supplies information from a different area; for example, when a workflow is evaluating the rules inside a rule set, we will see diagnostic information coming from the `System.Workflow.Activities.Rules` trace source.

We can configure each trace source with a value indicating the amount of information we need. The available values are `Critical`, `Error`, `Warning`, `Information`, and `All`. A value of `All` tells the trace source to give us every available bit of trace information. A value of `Critical` tells the trace source to publish only information about critical errors.

The last entry inside this section (`LogToFile`) is a trace switch that tells WF to send all trace output to a log file. The log file will have the name of `WorkflowTrace.log`, and will appear in the working directory of the application. The screenshot below shows the contents of the log file after running our sample code with the above configuration. Each line of output contains the trace source name and a textual message. In this sample, all trace information came from the `System.Workflow.Runtime` source.

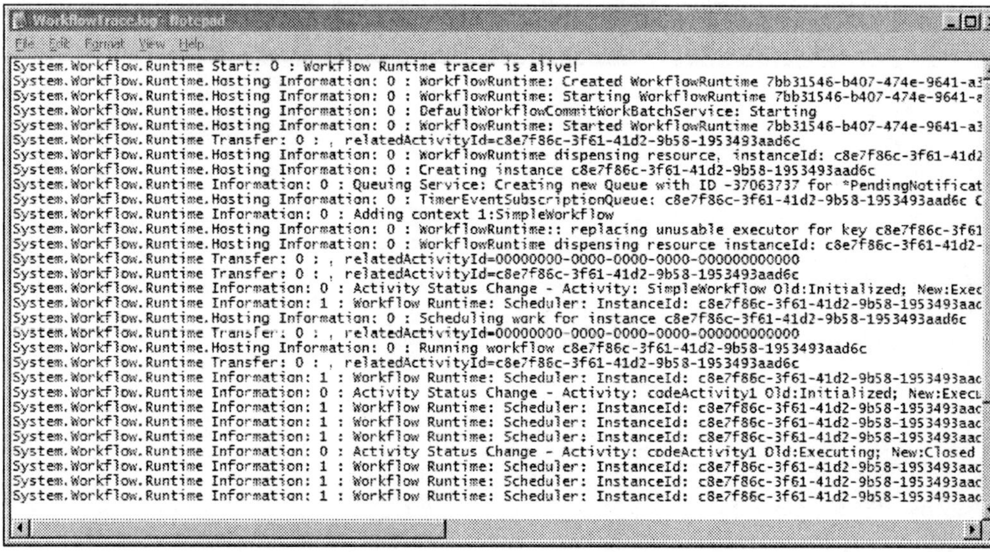

When we are inside the Visual Studio debugger, this trace information will also appear in the Output window of Visual Studio. If we want to send logging information to another destination, we can create a new **trace listener**. We can create trace listeners in the configuration file or in code. A trick for console-mode applications is to send trace information to the console with the following code:

```
TraceListener console;
console = new TextWriterTraceListener(Console.Out, "console");
Trace.Listeners.Add(console);

using(WorkflowRuntime runtime = new WorkflowRuntime())
using(AutoResetEvent reset = new AutoResetEvent(false))
{
```

```
      // ...run the workflow
  }
```

Before the above code will work we must configure the workflow runtime to send trace information to trace listeners. Placing the following XML inside the `<switches>` section will send trace information to all trace listeners.

```
<add name="System.Workflow LogToTraceListeners" value="1" />
```

Diagnostics and tracing aren't the only features of the runtime. We are now going to examine the configuration of services inside the runtime.

Workflow Runtime Configuration

There is an imperative approach to adding services to the runtime, and a declarative approach:

- The declarative approach configures services using the application's configuration file.
- The imperative approach creates services in code and adds them to the runtime with the `AddService` method of the `WorkflowRuntime` class.

We'll see examples of both approaches, but let's look at details of the declarative approach.

Workflow Configuration Sections

In the .NET configuration system, different **section handlers** manage different sections of the configuration file. WF provides the `WorkflowRuntimeSection` class to handle its specialized configuration section. What follows is a skeleton configuration file that configures a section handler and provides a section to initialize the WF runtime.

```
<?xml version="1.0" encoding="utf-8" ?>
<configuration>

  <configSections>
    <section
      name="MyRuntime"
      type="System.Workflow.Runtime.Configuration.
            WorkflowRuntimeSection, System.Workflow.Runtime,
            Version=3.0.00000.0, Culture=neutral,
            PublicKeyToken=31bf3856ad364e35"/>
  </configSections>

  <MyRuntime>
```

```
      <CommonParameters>
         <!-- add parameters used by all services -->
      </CommonParameters>
      <Services>
         <!-- add services -->
      </Services>
   </MyRuntime>

</configuration>
```

In the configuration listing above, we've assigned the WorkflowRuntimeSection class as a section handler for the MyRuntime section. This assignment takes place inside the <configSections> element. When the .NET runtime needs to read the MyRuntime section, it will instantiate a WorkflowRuntimeSection to do the work.

The MyRuntime section contains the actual workflow runtime configuration. A workflow configuration section contains two child nodes. The CommonParameters node holds name and value pairs that will be available to all the workflow services. If we have multiple services that need the same database connection string, we can add the connection string once inside CommonParameters instead of copying the string for each individual service. The Services node in this section contains the service types we add to the workflow runtime.

To have a workflow runtime pick up the correct configuration settings, we need to point the runtime at the right configuration section. We do this by passing the section name as a parameter to the constructor of the WorkflowRuntime class. The code below will initialize the runtime with the configuration settings in the MyRuntime section.

```
WorkflowRuntime runtime = new WorkflowRuntime("MyRuntime")
```

 We can place multiple workflow configuration sections inside of a configuration file. Each section will need a section handler defined with a name attribute that matches the element name of a workflow configuration section. The type attribute for the section handler is always the fully qualified name of WorkflowRuntimeSection class.

It's possible to start more than one workflow runtime inside an application. We can configure each runtime differently by providing multiple configuration sections. The ability to use multiple runtimes is useful when workflows need different execution environments. We'll see an example in the next section when we talk about the workflow scheduling services.

Scheduling Services

Scheduling services in WF are responsible for arranging workflows onto threads for execution. The two scheduling services provided by WF are the DefaultWorkflowSchedulerService and the ManualWorkflowSchedulerService. If we don't explicitly configure a scheduling service, the runtime will use the default scheduler (DefaultWorkflowSchedulerService). Both classes derive from the WorkflowSchedulerService class. We can derive our own class from this base class and override its virtual methods if we need custom scheduling logic.

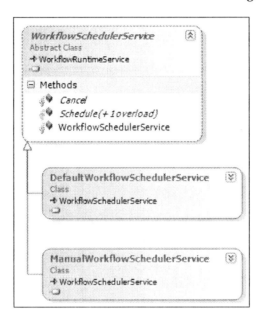

The workflow runtime invokes the Schedule and Cancel methods to plan workflow execution. The default scheduling service will schedule workflows to run on threads from the process-wide CLR thread pool. This is why workflows execute asynchronously on a background thread by default, and why our example waits for the workflow to finish by blocking the main thread with an AutoResetEvent. A host using the manual scheduling service must donate threads to the workflow runtime. The runtime will use a donated thread to execute a workflow. We can use the manual scheduling service to execute workflows synchronously.

Scheduling Services and Threads

Let's take a simple workflow with a single code activity inside. The code activity will invoke the only method in our code-behind class, shown overleaf.

```
public partial class SimpleWorkflow : SequentialWorkflowActivity
{
    private void codeActivity1_ExecuteCode(object sender,
                                           EventArgs e)
    {
        Console.WriteLine("Hello from {0}", this.QualifiedName);
        Console.WriteLine("  I am running on thread {0}",
            Thread.CurrentThread.ManagedThreadId);
    }
}
```

To see the difference between the two scheduling services, we will run the simple
workflow once with the manual scheduler, and once with the default scheduler. The
following code will replace the sample workflow driver we wrote earlier. In this
example, we are adding the scheduling services to the workflow runtime using code
(the imperative configuration approach).

```
WorkflowRuntime runtime1 = new WorkflowRuntime();
WorkflowRuntime runtime2 = new WorkflowRuntime();

ManualWorkflowSchedulerService scheduler;
scheduler = new ManualWorkflowSchedulerService();
runtime1.AddService(scheduler);

WorkflowInstance instance;
instance = runtime1.CreateWorkflow(typeof(SimpleWorkflow));

Console.WriteLine("Setting up workflow from thread {0}",
    Thread.CurrentThread.ManagedThreadId);

instance.Start();
scheduler.RunWorkflow(instance.InstanceId);

instance = runtime2.CreateWorkflow(typeof(SimpleWorkflow));
instance.Start();
```

We have two workflow runtimes active in this example. We configure `runtime1` to
use the manual workflow scheduler. We don't explicitly configure `runtime2` with
a scheduler, so this runtime will use the default scheduler. Our code prints out the
current thread ID before executing any workflows.

Notice how running a workflow with the manual scheduler is a two-step process.
First, we must schedule the workflow to run by calling `Start` on the workflow
instance. Calling `Start` only prepares the runtime for this instance and does
not actually run the workflow. To have the workflow execute we explicitly call
`RunWorkflow` on the manual scheduling service and pass an instance ID. The manual
service will use the calling thread to execute the workflow synchronously. This is
how a host donates a thread.

With the default scheduling service in runtime2, we only need to call Start on our workflow instance. The default scheduler will automatically queue the workflow to run on a thread from the thread pool. We can see the different threads by running the program and observing the output. When using runtime1 the workflow will execute on the same thread as the calling program. When using runtime2 the workflow will execute on a different thread.

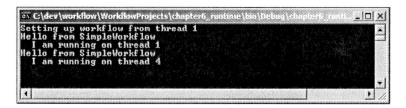

Scheduling Services and Configuration

One advantage to configuring our runtimes using the application configuration file is that we can change services and service parameters without recompiling an application. Let's see what our last program might look like if we used the following configuration file:

```xml
<?xml version="1.0" encoding="utf-8" ?>
<configuration>
  <configSections>
    <section
      name="ManualRuntime"
      type="System.Workflow.Runtime.Configuration.
            WorkflowRuntimeSection,System.Workflow.Runtime,
            Version=3.0.00000.0, Culture=neutral,
            PublicKeyToken=31bf3856ad364e35"/>
    <section
      name="DefaultRuntime"
      type="System.Workflow.Runtime.Configuration.
            WorkflowRuntimeSection, System.Workflow.Runtime,
            Version=3.0.00000.0, Culture=neutral,
          PublicKeyToken=31bf3856ad364e35"/>
  </configSections>

  <ManualRuntime>
    <Services>
      <add type= "System.Workflow.Runtime.Hosting.
                  ManualWorkflowSchedulerService,
                  System.Workflow.Runtime, Version=3.0.00000.0,
                  Culture=neutral, PublicKeyToken=31bf3856ad364e35"
```

```
                      useActiveTimers="true"/>
      </Services>
    </ManualRuntime>

    <DefaultRuntime>
      <Services>
        <add type="System.Workflow.Runtime.Hosting.
                    DefaultWorkflowSchedulerService,
                    System.Workflow.Runtime, Version=3.0.00000.0,
                    Culture=neutral, PublicKeyToken=31bf3856ad364e35"
                    maxSimultaneousWorkflows="3" />
      </Services>
    </DefaultRuntime>
  </configuration>
```

Notice we have two workflow configuration sections with a section handler for
each section. The `ManualRuntime` section configures the manual scheduler and
the `DefaultRuntime` section configures the default scheduler. Each service has an
additional configuration parameter. We'll return to discuss these parameters. We
must change our code to use this configuration file.

```
WorkflowRuntime runtime1 = new WorkflowRuntime("ManualRuntime");
WorkflowRuntime runtime2 = new WorkflowRuntime("DefaultRuntime");

WorkflowInstance instance;
instance = runtime1.CreateWorkflow(typeof(SimpleWorkflow));

Console.WriteLine("Setting up workflow from thread {0}",
    Thread.CurrentThread.ManagedThreadId);

instance.Start();

ManualWorkflowSchedulerService scheduler;
scheduler = runtime1.GetService<ManualWorkflowSchedulerService>();
scheduler.RunWorkflow(instance.InstanceId);

instance = runtime2.CreateWorkflow(typeof(SimpleWorkflow));
instance.Start();
```

This code initializes each runtime by passing in a configuration section name. The
primary difference in this code is how we obtain a reference to the manual scheduling
service. Since we didn't create the instance explicitly, we need to ask the runtime for a
reference. The generic `GetService` method of the `WorkflowRuntime` class will find and
return the service with a type matching the generic type parameter.

Scheduling Parameters

Each scheduling service has a parameter to tweak its behavior. The manual scheduler has a `useActiveTimers` parameter we can set in the configuration file, or pass as a parameter to the service's constructor. When `useActiveTimers` is false (the default), the host is responsible for resuming workflows after any `DelayActivity` expires. When the parameter is true, the service will set up a background thread and use in-memory timers to resume workflow execution automatically.

The default scheduler has a `maxSimultaneousWorkflows` parameter. This parameter controls the maximum number of workflow instances running concurrently in the thread pool. The default value on a uni-processor machine is 5, and on a multi-processor machine is 5 * `Environment.ProcessorCount` * 0.8.

The processes-wide CLR thread pool has an upper limit on the number of worker threads it will create. The default maximum is 25 * the number of processors on the machine. For applications running a high volume of workflows, tweaking the `maxSimultaneousWorkflows` parameter might be necessary to achieve a balance between workflow throughput and the availability of free threads in the thread pool. Starving the thread pool by having the workflow runtime use too many threads can result in deadlocks and application hangs.

Choosing the Right Scheduling Service

With two scheduling services available, an obvious question is — which scheduling service is the right service to use? Most smart client applications will work well with the default scheduling service. Applications written with Windows Forms and Windows Presentation Foundation technologies will want to execute workflows asynchronously on thread-pool threads and keep the user interface responsive.

Server-side applications generally work differently. A server application wants to process the maximum number of client requests using as few threads as possible. The ASP.NET runtime in web applications and web services already processes HTTP requests using threads from the thread pool. The asynchronous execution of workflows using the default scheduler would only tie up an additional thread per request. Server-side applications will generally want to use the manual scheduler and donate the request thread for workflow execution.

Persistence Services

Persistence services solve the problems inherent in executing long-running workflows. Many business processes take days, weeks, and months to complete. We can't keep workflow instances in memory while waiting for the accountant to return from the beaches of Spain and approve an expense report.

Long-running workflows spend the majority of their time in an idle state. The workflow might be idle waiting for a `Delay` activity to finish, or for an event to arrive in a `HandleExternalEvent` activity. When a persistence service is available, the runtime can persist and then unload an idle workflow. Persistence saves the state of the workflow into long-term storage. When the event finally arrives, the runtime can restore the workflow and resume processing.

The workflow runtime decides when to persist workflows, and the persistence service decides *how* and *where* to save the workflow state. The runtime will ask the persistence service to save a workflow's state when a workflow goes idle. An idle workflow is a workflow that has no activities to execute and is waiting for external events to arrive or delay activities to expire. The runtime will also ask the persistence service to save a workflow's state when the workflow reaches the following conditions.

- When an atomic transaction inside a `TransactionScope` activity or `CompensatableTransactionScopeActivity` activity completes
- When the host application calls the `Unload` or `RequestPersist` methods on a `WorkflowInstance` object
- When a custom activity with the `PersistOnClose` attribute completes
- When a `CompensatableSequence` activity completes
- When a workflow terminates or completes

The last condition might be surprising. A terminated or completed workflow can't perform any more work so there would be no need to reload the workflow. However, a persistence service can use the opportunity to clean up workflow state left behind from previous operations. A persistence service that saves workflow state into a database record, for instance, could delete the record when the workflow is finished executing. Alternatively, a persistence service could save the workflow state to use for audit purposes at some time in the future.

Persistence Classes

All persistence services derive from the `WorkflowPersistenceService` class. This class defines abstract methods we need to implement if we write a custom persistence service. The abstract methods of the class appear in italics in the screenshot on the next page. The base class also provides some concrete methods for a derived class to use. `GetDefaultSerializedForm`, for instance, accepts an `Activity` as a parameter and returns an array of bytes representing the serialized activity. To serialize an entire workflow we would need to pass the root activity of the workflow to this method.

Windows Workflow provides one persistence service out of the box — the `SqlWorkflowPersistenceService`. The SQL persistence service saves workflow state into a Microsoft SQL Server database and is the focus for the rest of this section.

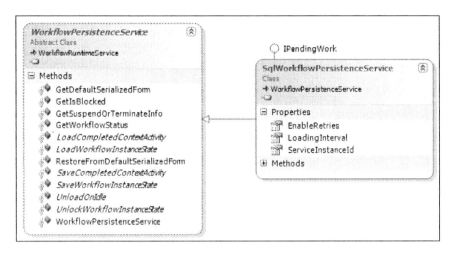

The SqlWorkflowPersistenceService

To get started with the SQL persistence service we'll need a database. We can use an existing database, or we can create a new database using Enterprise Manager, Query Analyzer, or the new SQL Server Management Studio for SQL Server 2005. We can also use the command-line `sqlcmd.exe` (for SQL Server 2005), or `osql.exe` (for SQL Server 2000).

Once a database is in place, we'll need to run the Windows Workflow SQL persistence scripts, which create the database objects needed by the persistence service. We can find these scripts underneath the Windows Workflow installation directory. Since WF is installed as part of the .NET 3.0 runtime, the location will look like `C:\WINDOWS\Microsoft.NET\Framework\v3.0\Windows Workflow Foundation\SQL\EN`.

The SQL scripts are `SqlPersistenceService_Schema.sql` and `SqlPersistenceService_Logic.sql`. We need to run the schema file first. The schema file will create the tables and indexes in the database. The logic file creates a handful of stored procedures for the persistence service to use. The screenshot overleaf demonstrates how we can set up a persistence database using `sqlcmd.exe`. We first create a database, and then run the two script files using the `:r` command of `sqlcmd.exe`.

```
Windows PowerShell                                              _ |□| x|
PS C:\> sqlcmd
1> create database WorkflowDB
2> go
1> use WorkflowDB
2> go
Changed database context to 'WorkflowDB'.
1> :r "c:\windows\microsoft.net\framework\v3.0\windows workflow foundation\sql\e
n\sqlpersistenceservice_schema.sql"
1> :r "c:\windows\microsoft.net\framework\v3.0\windows workflow foundation\sql\e
n\sqlpersistenceservice_logic.sql"
DBCC execution completed. If DBCC printed error messages, contact your system ad
ministrator.
1> exit
PS C:\>
```

SQL Persistence Service Configuration

Once we have a database with the persistence schema and logic inside, we can add
the persistence service to the workflow runtime. We'll add the service declaratively
using the following configuration file:

```xml
<?xml version="1.0" encoding="utf-8" ?>
<configuration>

  <configSections>
    <section
      name="WorkflowWithPersistence"
      type="System.Workflow.Runtime.Configuration.
            WorkflowRuntimeSection, System.Workflow.Runtime,
            Version=3.0.00000.0, Culture=neutral,
            PublicKeyToken=31bf3856ad364e35"/>
  </configSections>

  <WorkflowWithPersistence>
    <CommonParameters>
      <add name="ConnectionString"
           value="Data Source=(local);Initial Catalog=WorkflowDB;
                               Integrated Security=true"/>
    </CommonParameters>
    <Services>
      <add type="System.Workflow.Runtime.Hosting.
                 SqlWorkflowPersistenceService,
                 System.Workflow.Runtime, Version=3.0.00000.0,
                 Culture=neutral, PublicKeyToken=31bf3856ad364e35"
           UnloadOnIdle="true" />
    </Services>
  </WorkflowWithPersistence>

</configuration>
```

We've added the database connection string under `CommonParameters`. This will allow us to share the connection string with other services that require database connectivity. The `SqlWorkflowPersistenceService` appears underneath the `Services` node. There are parameters available to fine-tune the behavior of the service. We've attached one parameter in this example — the `UnloadOnIdle` parameter. The available parameters are shown in the table below:

Parameter Name	Description
EnableRetries	When true, the service will retry failed database operations up to 20 times or until the operation completes successfully. The default is false.
LoadIntervalSeconds	How often the service will check for expired timers. The default is 120 seconds.
OwnershipTimeoutSeconds	When the persistence service loads a workflow, it will lock the workflow record for this length of time (important when multiple runtimes share the same persistence database). The default value is TimeSpan. MaxValue.
UnloadOnIdle	When true, the service will persist idle workflows. The default is false.

Running with Persistence

To see the persistence service in action, let's use the following workflow definition:

```
<SequentialWorkflowActivity
    x:Class="WorkflowWithDelay"
    x:Name="WorkflowWithDelay"
    xmlns:x="http://schemas.microsoft.com/winfx/2006/xaml"
    xmlns="http://schemas.microsoft.com/winfx/2006/xaml/workflow">

  <CodeActivity x:Name="codeActivity1"
              ExecuteCode="codeActivity_ExecuteCode" />
  <DelayActivity x:Name="delayActivity1"
              TimeoutDuration="00:00:10" />
  <CodeActivity x:Name="codeActivity2"
              ExecuteCode="codeActivity_ExecuteCode" />

</SequentialWorkflowActivity>
```

We have a `Delay` activity between two `Code` activities. The delay will idle the workflow for 10 seconds. The `ExecuteCode` events of both `Code` activities reference the same event handler in our code-behind class, listed overleaf. The event handler will write a simple message to the console window.

```
public partial class WorkflowWithDelay : SequentialWorkflowActivity
{
  private void codeActivity_ExecuteCode(object sender, EventArgs e)
  {
    CodeActivity activity = sender as CodeActivity;
    Console.WriteLine("Hello from {0}", activity.Name);
  }
}
```

Next, we'll put together a host to run the workflow. We'll subscribe to various events and print messages to track the progress of our workflow.

```
public class Persist
{
  public static void Run()
  {
    using(WorkflowRuntime runtime =
      new WorkflowRuntime("WorkflowWithPersistence"))
    using (AutoResetEvent reset =
      new AutoResetEvent(false))
    {
      runtime.WorkflowCompleted += delegate { reset.Set(); };
      runtime.WorkflowTerminated += delegate { reset.Set(); };

      runtime.WorkflowPersisted +=
        new EventHandler<WorkflowEventArgs>(
                          runtime_WorkflowPersisted);
      runtime.WorkflowLoaded +=
        new EventHandler<WorkflowEventArgs>(
                          runtime_WorkflowLoaded);
      runtime.WorkflowUnloaded +=
        new EventHandler<WorkflowEventArgs>(
                          runtime_WorkflowUnloaded);
      runtime.WorkflowIdled +=
        new EventHandler<WorkflowEventArgs>(
                          runtime_WorkflowIdled);

      WorkflowInstance instance;
      instance = runtime.CreateWorkflow(typeof(WorkflowWithDelay));
      instance.Start();
      reset.WaitOne();
    }
  }

  static void runtime_WorkflowIdled(object sender,
                                    WorkflowEventArgs e)
```

```
    {
      Console.WriteLine("Workflow {0} idled",
                        e.WorkflowInstance.InstanceId);
    }

    static void runtime_WorkflowUnloaded(object sender,
                                         WorkflowEventArgs e)
    {
      Console.WriteLine("Workflow {0} unloaded",
                        e.WorkflowInstance.InstanceId);
    }

    static void runtime_WorkflowLoaded(object sender,
                                       WorkflowEventArgs e)
    {
      Console.WriteLine("Workflow {0} loaded",
                        e.WorkflowInstance.InstanceId);
    }

    static void runtime_WorkflowPersisted(object sender,
                                          WorkflowEventArgs e)
    {
      Console.WriteLine("Workflow {0} persisted",
                        e.WorkflowInstance.InstanceId);
    }
  }
}
```

Our host application creates a new runtime, passing the name of the configuration section with the persistence configuration. The application subscribes to a number of workflow events that will print simple messages to the console. When we run the above code, we'll see the output as shown in the screenshot below:

The first `Code` activity runs and the prints a message to the screen. The `Delay` then blocks the workflow. The runtime sees the workflow has no work to perform and raises the `WorkflowIdled` event. The runtime also sees there is a persistence service available, and the service has specified `UnloadOnIdle`. The runtime asks the persistence service to save the state of the workflow, and then unloads the workflow instance. When the delay timer expires, the runtime uses the persistence service to reload the workflow instance and resumes the workflow's execution.

When the SQL persistence service reloads the workflow, the service will set a flag in the database to mark the instance as locked. If another persistence service in another process or on another machine tries to load the locked workflow instance, the service will raise an exception. The lock prevents this workflow instance from executing twice in two different runtimes. The lock is released when the workflow persists again, or when the lock timeout (specified by `OwnershipTimeoutSeconds`) expires.

When the workflow completes, the runtime again asks the persistence service to persist the workflow. The `SqlWorkflowPersistenceService` inspects the state of the workflow and sees the workflow is finished executing. The service will delete the previously saved state record instead of saving state. Most of the database work takes place in the `InstanceState` table of the persistence database.

In order for the persistence service to save the state of a workflow, it first has to serialize the workflow. Let's take a look at serialization in WF to get a better understanding of how persistence services will work.

Persistence and Serialization

There are two types of serialization in Windows Workflow. The runtime provides the `WorkflowMarkupSerializer` class to transform workflows into XAML. There is no need for the mark-up serializer to save the state, or data inside of a workflow. The goal of the mark-up serializer is to produce a *workflow definition* in XML for design tools and code generators.

Persistence services, on the other hand, use the `GetDefaultSerializedForm` method of the `WorkflowPersistenceService` base class. This method calls the public `Save` method of the Activity class, and the `Save` method uses a `BinaryFormatter` object to serialize a workflow. The binary formatter produces a byte stream, and the `WorkflowPersistenceService` runs the byte stream through a `GZipStream` for compression. The goal of binary serialization is to produce a compact representation of the *workflow instance* for long-term storage. There are two types of serialization in Windows Workflow because each type achieves different goals.

It's not important to understand all of the gritty serialization details. What is important to take away from the above paragraph is that the runtime uses the `BinaryFormatter` class from the base class library when persisting workflows. We need to keep this in mind if we write a workflow like the following:

```
public partial class WorkflowWithDelay2 : SequentialWorkflowActivity
{
  Bug _bug = new Bug();
}

class Bug
{
  private Guid _id;
  public Guid BugID
  {
    get { return _id; }
    set { _id = value; }
  }
}
```

Let's assume this workflow has a `Delay` activity inside, just as in our previous example. This workflow also includes a private `Bug` object. Although we don't do anything interesting with the `Bug` object, it will change our persistence behavior. If we run the workflow *without* a persistence service, the workflow should complete successfully. If we run the workflow *with* a persistence service, we'll see an exception similar to **Type Bug is not marked as serializable**.

The `BinaryFormatter` will attempt to serialize every piece of state information inside our workflow, including a custom object like our `Bug` object. When any object formatter comes across an object it needs to serialize, it first looks to see if there is a surrogate selector registered for the object's type. If no surrogate selector is available, the formatter checks to see if the `Type` is marked with the `Serializable` attribute. If neither of these conditions are met, the formatter will give up and throw an exception. Since we own the `Bug` class, we can decorate the `Bug` class with a `Serializable` attribute and avoid the exception.

```
[Serializable]
class Bug
{
  private Guid _id;
  public Guid BugID
  {
    get { return _id; }
    set { _id = value; }
  }
}
```

If some third party owns the `Bug` class, we can write a surrogate selector for serialization, which is beyond the scope of this chapter (see the `SurrogateSelector` class in the `System.Runtime.Serialization` namespace).

If there is a field that we don't need to serialize and restore with the workflow instance, we can tell the formatter to skip serialization with the `NonSerialized` attribute. The `Bug` object in the code below won't exist in the persisted form of the workflow. When the runtime reloads the workflow after a persistence point, the `_bug` field will be left unassigned.

```
public partial class WorkflowWithDelay2 : SequentialWorkflowActivity
{
    [NonSerialized]
    Bug _bug = new Bug();
}
```

A persistence service stores the state of a workflow and allows us to have workflows that survive machine restarts and run for months at a time. However, a persistence service cannot tell us what happened during the execution of a workflow, or how far along a workflow has progressed. Our next topic — tracking services, will give us this information.

Tracking Services

Windows Workflow provides extensible and scalable tracking features to capture and record information about workflow execution. A tracking service uses a **tracking profile** to filter the information it receives about a workflow. The WF runtime can send information about workflow events, activity state changes, rule evaluations, and our own custom instrumentation data. The tracking service decides what it will do with the data it receives. The service could write tracking data to a log file, or save the data in a database. The tracking service can participate in transactions with the workflow runtime to ensure the information it records is consistent and durable.

You might wonder how tracking information is different from the trace information we saw earlier in the chapter. Both features expose detailed information about important events inside the workflow runtime. However, tracking information is exposed through an API specialized for Windows Workflow. We'll also see in this section how tracking information can be saved to a database and later queried through the API provided by WF.

Tracking information sounds like a useful feature for system administrators who want to analyze resource usage, but there are also tremendous business scenarios for tracking information. For example, a company could use recorded tracking information to count the number of open invoices, or the average time for invoices to close. By measuring the tracking information, a business could improve its processes.

Tracking Classes

All tracking services derive from a `TrackingService` base class. This class defines the API for working with tracking profiles and **tracking channels**. As we mentioned earlier, a tracking profile defines and filters the type of information we want to receive from the runtime. A tracking channel is a communications conduit between the workflow runtime and the tracking service. The runtime will ask the service to give it a tracking channel based on profile information. Once the runtime has an open channel, it sends information to the service via the channel. If we write a custom tracking service, we'll also need to provide channels for the service.

Windows Workflow provides one implementation of a tracking service with the `SqlTrackingService` class. The `SqlTrackingService` writes the tracking information it receives to a SQL Server database. The `SqlTrackingService` also stores tracking profiles in the database.

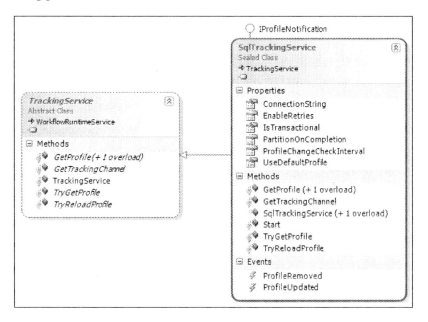

Just as we needed a schema for the SQL persistence service, we'll need to install the schema for the SQL tracking service. We can create the tracking schema in the same database as the persistence schema. The scripts to create the tracking schema are underneath the same directory as the persistence scripts (typically `C:\WINDOWS\Microsoft.NET\Framework\v3.0\Windows Workflow Foundation\SQL`). The scripts are `Tracking_Schema.sql`, and `Tracking_Logic.sql`. We must run the schema file before the logic file. Using the command-line tool to run the scripts would look as shown in the screenshot on the next page.

Tracking Configuration

We can configure a tracking service into our runtime either programmatically or with the application configuration file. The following configuration file will load the SQL tracking service with default parameters:

```xml
<?xml version="1.0" encoding="utf-8" ?>
<configuration>

  <configSections>
    <section
      name="WorkflowWithTracking"
      type="System.Workflow.Runtime.Configuration.
            WorkflowRuntimeSection,
            System.Workflow.Runtime, Version=3.0.00000.0,
            Culture=neutral, PublicKeyToken=31bf3856ad364e35"/>
  </configSections>

  <WorkflowWithTracking>
    <CommonParameters>
      <add name="ConnectionString"
           value="Data Source=(local);Initial Catalog=WorkflowDB;
                         Integrated Security=true"/>
    </CommonParameters>
    <Services>
      <add
        type="System.Workflow.Runtime.Tracking.SqlTrackingService,
              System.Workflow.Runtime, Version=3.0.00000.0,
              Culture=neutral,PublicKeyToken=31bf3856ad364e35"
           />
    </Services>
  </WorkflowWithTracking>
</configuration>
```

The parameters we can pass to the service are listed in the table below:

Name	Description
ConnectionString	The connection string to the tracking database.
EnableRetries	When true, the service will retry failed database operations up to 20 times or until the operation completes successfully. The default is false.
IsTransactional	When true, the service will participate in transactions with the workflow runtime and other services, like the persistence service. The default is true.
PartitionOnCompletion	For high uptime and scalability, the partitioning feature periodically creates a new set of tables to store information about completed workflow instances. The default value is false.
ProfileChangeCheckInterval	The service caches tracking profiles but will periodically poll to see if there is a change. The default poll interval is 1 minute.
UseDefaultProfile	When true, the service will return a default tracking profile if no profile is defined. The default is true.

Running with Tracking

With the tracking service added in the configuration file, there is nothing special we need to do at run time. The code we use to run a workflow with tracking is the same as it has always been.

```
static public void RunSimple()
{
  using (WorkflowRuntime runtime =
    new WorkflowRuntime("WorkflowWithTracking"))
  using (AutoResetEvent reset = new AutoResetEvent(false))
  {
    runtime.WorkflowCompleted += delegate { reset.Set(); };
    runtime.WorkflowTerminated += delegate { reset.Set(); };

    WorkflowInstance instance;
    instance = runtime.CreateWorkflow(typeof(SimpleWorkflow));
    instance.Start();
    reset.WaitOne();

    DumpTrackingEvents(instance.InstanceId);
  }
}
```

When the program finishes we'll have a great deal of information recorded across several tables in our SQL Server tracking database. We can use some handwritten queries to examine the tracking information, or we can use one of many views the tracking schema installs in the database. There is also a complete object model for us to query tracking information programmatically. The classes we can use are shown in the screenshot below:

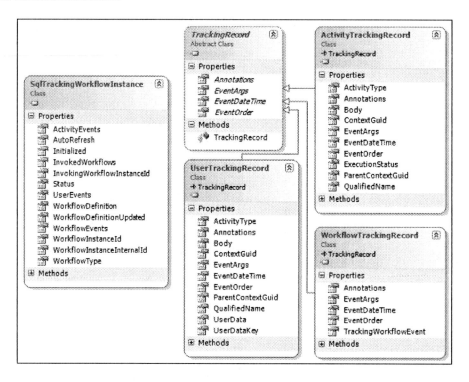

The `SqlTrackingWorkflowInstance` class gives us access to tracking information about a specific workflow instance. The `ActivityEvents` property of the class will return a list of `ActivityTrackingRecord` objects. Likewise, the `WorkflowEvents` property will return `WorkflowTrackingRecord` objects, and the `UserEvents` property will return `UserTrackingRecord` objects (which are custom events we can define). Notice the breadth of information includes time stamps, arguments, and status codes. The class even includes a `WorkflowDefinition` property that will return a XAML definition of the workflow. This feature can be useful for auditing workflows that use dynamic updates or that we customize for each client.

The code on the next page makes use of these classes to retrieve a subset of the tracking information. Given a connection string and a workflow instance ID, the `SqlTrackingQuery` class can return a `SqlTrackingWorkflowInstance` object, which gives us access to all the records. The connection string we can read from the application configuration file, while the instance ID we will receive as a parameter.

```
public static void DumpTrackingEvents(Guid instanceID)
{
  WorkflowRuntimeSection config;
  config = ConfigurationManager.GetSection("WorkflowWithTracking")
        as WorkflowRuntimeSection;

  SqlTrackingQuery query = new SqlTrackingQuery();
  query.ConnectionString =
    config.CommonParameters["ConnectionString"].Value;


  SqlTrackingWorkflowInstance trackingInstace;
  query.TryGetWorkflow(instanceID, out trackingInstace);
  if (trackingInstace != null)
  {
    Console.WriteLine("Tracking Information for {0}", instanceID);

    Console.WriteLine("    Workflow Events");
    foreach(WorkflowTrackingRecord r in trackingInstace.
WorkflowEvents)
    {
      Console.WriteLine("    Date: {0}, Status: {1}",
                    r.EventDateTime, r.TrackingWorkflowEvent);
    }

    Console.WriteLine("  Activity Events");
    foreach (ActivityTrackingRecord r in trackingInstace.
ActivityEvents)
    {
      Console.WriteLine("    Activity: {0} Date: {1} Status: {2}",
         r.QualifiedName, r.EventDateTime, r.ExecutionStatus);

    }
  }
}
```

The output of this code is shown in the screenshot below:

Running one simple workflow produced a vast amount of tracking information (we've seen only a subset in this example). The SQL tracking service provided a default tracking profile that took all the information the runtime produced. If we only want to track specific pieces of information, we'll need a custom tracking profile.

Tracking Profiles

When the workflow runtime creates a new workflow instance, it will call `TryGetProfile` on each running tracking service and pass the workflow instance as a parameter. If a tracking profile has been configured for the workflow type, the `TryGetProfile` method will return an output parameter of type `TrackingProfile`. The runtime filters the tracking information it sends to the service using **track points** defined in the profile. The classes involved in building a tracking profile are shown in the screenshot below:

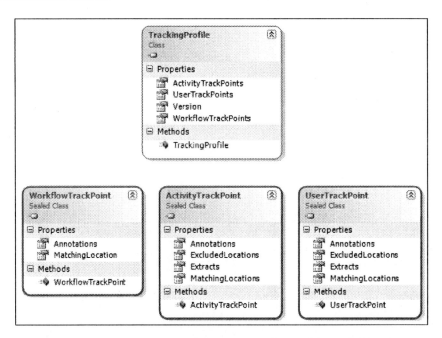

Let's say we don't want to track the individual activities inside a workflow. Instead, we want to track just information about the workflow itself. We'll need to define and create a new `TrackingProfile` object and populate the `WorkflowTrackPoints` property. We will leave the `ActivityTrackPoints` and `UserTrackPoints` properties empty.

```
TrackingProfile profile = new TrackingProfile();
profile.Version = new Version("1.0.0");
WorkflowTrackPoint workflowTrackPoint = new WorkflowTrackPoint();
```

```
Array statuses = Enum.GetValues(typeof(TrackingWorkflowEvent));
foreach (TrackingWorkflowEvent status in statuses)
{
  workflowTrackPoint.MatchingLocation.Events.Add(status);
}
profile.WorkflowTrackPoints.Add(workflowTrackPoint);

string profileAsXml = SerializeProfile(profile);
UpdateTrackingProfile(profileAsXml);
```

A tracking profile needs a version. Tracking services will cache profiles to avoid re-fetching them each time the runtime asks for the profile. If we update a profile, we need to change the version in order for the tracking service to recognize the update.

The code above populates the `WorkflowTrackPoints` collection with the workflow event types we want to record. By using `Enum.GetValues` on the `TrackingWorkflowEvent` enumeration, we will get all possible events, which includes `Started`, `Completed`, `Persisted`, and `Terminated`, among others.

Once we've populated the `TrackingProfile` object, we need to update the profile in the tracking service. The first step in the update process is to serialize the profile object to XML. The `TrackingProfileSerializer` will perform the serialization for us.

```
private static string SerializeProfile(TrackingProfile profile)

{
  TrackingProfileSerializer serializer;
  serializer = new TrackingProfileSerializer();

  StringWriter writer = new StringWriter(new StringBuilder());
  serializer.Serialize(writer, profile);

  return writer.ToString();
}
```

The SQL tracking service stores profiles as XML in the `TrackingProfile` table (except for the default tracking profile, which the service keeps in the `DefaultTrackingProfile` table). The best approach for updating and inserting into this table is to use the `UpdateTrackingProfile` stored procedure. When we add a new tracking profile, we must associate the profile with a workflow type. We will associate the new profile with our `SimpleWorkflow` workflow.

```
private static void UpdateTrackingProfile(string profileAsXml)
{
  WorkflowRuntimeSection config;
  config = ConfigurationManager.GetSection("WorkflowWithTracking")
            as WorkflowRuntimeSection;
```

```
using (SqlConnection connection = new SqlConnection())
{
    connection.ConnectionString =
        config.CommonParameters["ConnectionString"].Value;

    SqlCommand command = new SqlCommand();
    command.Connection = connection;
    command.CommandType = CommandType.StoredProcedure;
    command.CommandText = "dbo.UpdateTrackingProfile";

    command.Parameters.Add(
        new SqlParameter("@TypeFullName",
            typeof(SimpleWorkflow).ToString()));

    command.Parameters.Add(
        new SqlParameter("@AssemblyFullName",
            typeof(SimpleWorkflow).Assembly.FullName));

    command.Parameters.Add(
        new SqlParameter("@Version","1.0.1"));

    command.Parameters.Add(
        new SqlParameter("@TrackingProfileXml", profileAsXml));

    connection.Open();
    command.ExecuteNonQuery();

}
}
```

There are four parameters to the UpdateTrackingProfile stored procedure. The @TypeFullName parameter needs the full type name (including namespace) of the workflow to associate with this profile. Likewise, the @AssemblyFullName parameter will need the full name of the assembly containing the associated workflow's definition. The @Version parameter should contain the version of the tracking profile, and the @TrackingProfileXml should contain the XML representation of a TrackingProfile object.

With the tracking profile in the database, we will record different information when we run our simple workflow. Other workflows will continue to use the default tracking profile which records every event. Rerunning our program shows the output in the screenshot on the next page. We are still recording workflow tracking events, but the profile we've defined doesn't record any activity events.

```
Hello from SimpleWorkflow
     I am running on thread 10
Tracking Information for 968cf426-a7f5-4852-90b7-5883c5bcd85e
   Workflow Events
     Date: 8/4/2006 5:17:41 PM, Status: Created
     Date: 8/4/2006 5:17:41 PM, Status: Started
     Date: 8/4/2006 5:17:42 PM, Status: Completed
   Activity Events
```

Data Maintenance

The SQL Tracking service provides a partitioning feature to move tracking information out of the primary set of tracking tables and into a set of partitioned tracking tables. This feature helps to manage the growth of tracking tables. Administrators can move and archive old tracking information, and the table used for the current partition will never grow excessively large.

When a partitioning takes place, a new set of partition tables will be created for each elapsed partition interval. The SetPartitionInterval stored procedure configures the partitioning interval. The default interval is monthly, but other valid values include daily, weekly, and yearly. The tables will contain the partition date as part of the table name.

There are two approaches to partitioning. Automatic partitioning is configured by setting the PartitionOnCompletion parameter of the SQL tracking service to true. Automatic partitioning will move tracking information into a partition as soon as a workflow completes. Automatic partitioning is good for applications that don't have any down time, but will add some overhead as completed workflow records constantly shuffle into partitions.

We can also use manual partitioning by running the PartitionCompletedWorkflowInstances stored procedure. The stored procedure will move tracking records for completed workflows into partitioned tables. For applications with some down time we could schedule this stored procedure to run during non-peak hours.

Persistence and Tracking Together

The SQL persistence and SQL tracking services work to provide durable storage for workflow state and workflow tracking information respectively. However, they don't quite work *together*. Specifically, each service will operate using different connections to the database. A workflow runtime with both services present will use more connections then necessary. Additional overhead will arise if the tracking service is transactional. When transactions span multiple connections, the Microsoft Distributed Transaction Coordinator (MSDTC) becomes involved and manages the transaction. MSDTC carries some overheard.

WF provides an optimization for applications using both the SQL persistence and SQL tracking services with the `SharedConnectionWorkflowCommitWorkBatchService` class. The service allows the two SQL services to share a connection if the connection string for both is the same.

Shared Connection Configuration

The configuration file below configures both SQL workflow services and the shared connection service. Since we define the connection string parameter in the `CommonParameters` section, all the services will use the same connection string.

```xml
<?xml version="1.0" encoding="utf-8" ?>
<configuration>

  <configSections>
    <section
      name="WorkflowConfiguration"
      type="System.Workflow.Runtime.Configuration.
            WorkflowRuntimeSection,
            System.Workflow.Runtime, Version=3.0.00000.0,
            Culture=neutral, PublicKeyToken=31bf3856ad364e35"/>
  </configSections>

  <WorkflowConfiguration>
    <CommonParameters>
      <add name="ConnectionString"
           value="Data Source=(local);Initial Catalog=WorkflowDB;
                                 Integrated Security=true"/>
    </CommonParameters>
    <Services>
      <add
        type="System.Workflow.Runtime.Tracking.
              SqlTrackingService,
              System.Workflow.Runtime, Version=3.0.00000.0,
              Culture=neutral, PublicKeyToken=31bf3856ad364e35"/>
      <add
        type="System.Workflow.Runtime.Hosting.
              SqlWorkflowPersistenceService,
              System.Workflow.Runtime, Version=3.0.00000.0,
              Culture=neutral, PublicKeyToken=31bf3856ad364e35"
              UnloadOnIdle="true" />
```

```
    <add
      type= "System.Workflow.Runtime.Hosting.
              SharedConnectionWorkflowCommitWorkBatchService,
              System.Workflow.Runtime, Version=3.0.00000.0,
              Culture=neutral, PublicKeyToken=31bf3856ad364e35" />
    </Services>
  </WorkflowConfiguration>
</configuration>
```

We don't need to change our application, as the shared connection service will coordinate behind the scenes with the other runtime services.

Summary

This chapter reviewed the capabilities of the Windows Workflow runtime. We examined how to monitor the workflow runtime by subscribing to runtime events and configuring tracing information. We also examined how to customize the runtime by adding services. These services include scheduling services (to manage threads), persistence services (to manage state), and tracking services (to record tracking information). If the built-in services do not fulfil our requirements, we can replace any of them with custom versions we write ourselves. This architecture gives the Windows Workflow runtime its flexibility and extensibility.

7
Event-Driven Workflows

There is one important decision to make when creating a new workflow. Will the workflow be a sequential workflow, or a state machine workflow? Windows Workflow provides these two workflow execution types out of the box. To answer the question, we have to decide *who* is in control.

A sequential workflow is a predictable workflow. The execution path might branch, or loop, or wait for an outside event to occur, but in the end, the sequential workflow will use the activities, conditions, and rules we've provided to march inevitably forward. The workflow is in control of the process.

A state machine workflow is an event-driven workflow. That is, the state machine workflow relies on external events to drive the workflow to completion. We define the legal states of the workflow, and the legal transitions between those states. The workflow is always in one of the states, and has to wait for an event to arrive before transitioning to a new state. Generally, the important decisions happen *outside* the workflow. The state machine defines a structure to follow, but control belongs to the outside world.

We use a sequential workflow when we can encode most of the decision-making inside the workflow itself. We use a state machine workflow when the decision-making happens outside the workflow. In this chapter, we will take a closer look at how state machines operate.

What Is a State Machine?

State machines have been around in computer science for a long time. You'll find they are especially popular in reactive systems, like the software for video games and robotics. Designers use state machines to model a system using states, events, and transitions.

A **state** represents a situation or circumstance. In the screenshot below, we have a state machine with two states: a **Power On** state and a **Power Off** state. The machine will always be in one of these two states.

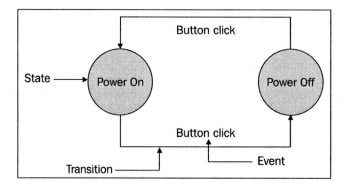

An **event** is some outside stimulus. In the screenshot above, we only have one type of event, a button-click event. The state machine will respond to this event in either the **Power On** or the **Power Off** state. Not all states have to respond to the same events.

A **transition** moves the state machine to the next state. A transition can only occur in response to an event. Transitions don't have to move the state machine to a new state—a transition could loop back to the same state. When the machine receives a button-click event in the **Power Off** state, it transitions to the **Power On** state. Conversely, if the machine is in the **Power On** state and receives a button-click event, it moves to the **Power Off** state.

Implied in the concept of a state transition is that some action will take place before or after the transition. That is, a state machine doesn't merely store state, it also executes code when events arrive. In the figure above, the state machine would be controlling the flow of electricity by opening or closing a circuit when it arrives in a new state.

State Machines in Windows Workflow

The state machine in the screenshot above is quite simple, and most systems will require a more sophisticated model. However, the concepts introduced in the screenshot (states, events, and transitions) are the same concepts we use to build state machine workflows in Windows Workflow.

In WF, the State activity represents a state in a state machine workflow. As events arrive, the workflow will transition between State activities. A state machine workflow must specify an initial state, which will be the starting state for the workflow. A state machine workflow can optionally specify a completed state. The workflow will conclude after it transitions to the completed state.

An `EventDriven` activity represents an event in a state machine. We place these activities inside `State` activities to represent the legal events for the state. Inside an `EventDriven` activity, we can place a sequence of activities that will execute when the event arrives. The last activity in the sequence is commonly a `SetState` activity. A `SetState` activity specifies a transition to the next state.

Our First State Machine

As detailed in Chapter 2, we can author workflows using code only, XAML only, or a combination of code and XAML (code-separation). State machine workflows are no different in this respect. We will build the workflows in this chapter using the code-separation approach, although any of the authoring modes would work.

Our workflow will support a bug-tracking application. Specifically, we will be tracking the life cycle of a software bug as the bug moves from an *Open* state to a *Closed* state. During its lifetime, a bug might also be in the *Assigned*, *Resolved*, and *Deferred* states.

Why use a state machine to model the workflow of bug fixes? Because is it impossible to model the choices a bug will need to reach a completed state. Think about the decision-making required at each step in a bug's life. A newly opened bug requires some evaluation. Is the bug a duplicate? Is the bug really a bug? Even if the bug really is a defect, not all defects move directly to someone's work queue. We must weigh the bug's severity against the project schedule and available resources to fix the bug. Since we can't put all of the intelligence we need into the workflow, we'll rely on external events to tell the workflow what decisions we've made.

Creating the Project

Our adventure starts, as most adventures do, with the **New Project** dialog box of Visual Studio (**File | New Project**). As shown in the screenshot overleaf, we will use the State Machine Workflow Console Mode application. The project template will set up a project with all the assembly references we need to program with Windows Workflow.

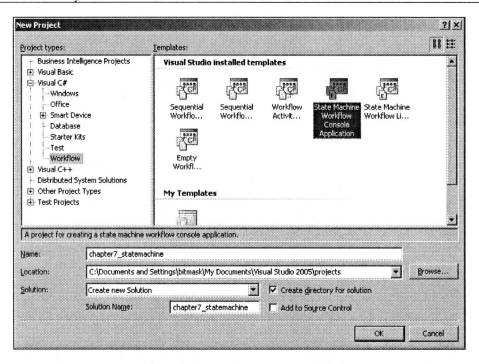

The new project will include a default workflow in a file named `Workflow1.cs`. We can delete this file and add our own **State Machine Workflow (with code separation)**, named `BugWorkflow.xoml` (see the screenshot below).

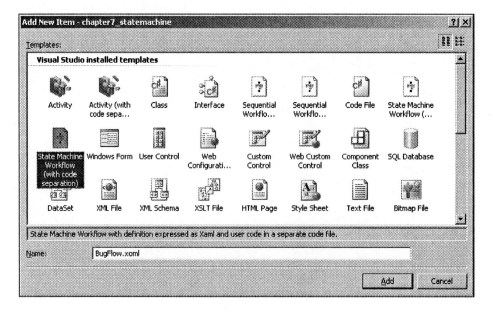

The workflow designer will appear with our new state machine workflow (see the screenshot below). At this point, the **Toolbox** window will be available and populated with activities from the base activity library. Initially, however, we can only use a subset of activity types — the activity types listed inside the `BugFlowInitialState` shape in the screenshot below:

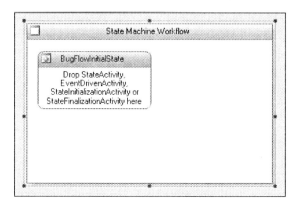

Before we can begin to design our state machine, we are going to need some supporting code. Specifically, we need a service that will provide the events to drive the workflow.

Life of a Bug

State machines will spend most of their time waiting for events to arrive from a local communication service. We know from our discussion of local communication services in Chapter 3 that we will need an interface that defines a service contract. The interface will define events that the service can raise to provide data to the workflow, and methods the workflow can invoke on the service. For this example, our communication is unidirectional — all we define is events.

```
[ExternalDataExchange]
public interface IBugService
{
    event EventHandler<BugStateChangedEventArgs> BugOpened;
    event EventHandler<BugStateChangedEventArgs> BugResolved;
    event EventHandler<BugStateChangedEventArgs> BugClosed;
    event EventHandler<BugStateChangedEventArgs> BugDeferred;
    event EventHandler<BugStateChangedEventArgs> BugAssigned;
}
```

The event arguments for these events will require the service to pass along information the workflow can use during processing. For example, one useful piece of information will be a `Bug` object that carries all the attributes (title, description, assignment) of a bug.

```
[Serializable]
public class BugStateChangedEventArgs : ExternalDataEventArgs
{
    public BugStateChangedEventArgs(Guid instanceID, Bug bug)
        : base(instanceID)
    {
        _bug = bug;
        WaitForIdle = true;
    }

    private Bug _bug;
    public Bug Bug
    {
        get { return _bug; }
        set { _bug = value; }
    }

}
```

The service that implements the `IBugService` interface will raise events when the status of a bug changes. For instance, the service might fire the event from a smart client application in response to a user manipulating the bug in the UI. Alternatively, the service might fire the event from an ASP.NET web service upon receiving updated bug information in a web service call. The point is that the workflow doesn't care why the event fires, and doesn't care about the decisions leading up to the event. The workflow only cares that the event happens.

We will use a naive implementation of the bug service interface and provide simple methods that raise events. Later in the chapter, we will use this service in a console-mode program to raise events to the workflow.

```
public class BugService : IBugService
{
    public event
        EventHandler<BugStateChangedEventArgs> BugOpened;
    public void OpenBug(Guid id, Bug bug)
    {
        if (BugOpened != null)
        {
            BugOpened(null,
                    new BugStateChangedEventArgs(id, bug));
        }
    }
```

```
    // and so on ...

}
```

Now that we know about the service contract our workflow will use, we can continue building our state machine.

The State Activity

The State activity represents a state in the state machine workflow. Not surprisingly, state activities are the backbone of event-driven workflows. We can generally start a workflow design by dropping all the State activities we need from the **Toolbox** window into the designer. If we drop a State activity for each possible state of a software bug, we'll have a designer view like that below:

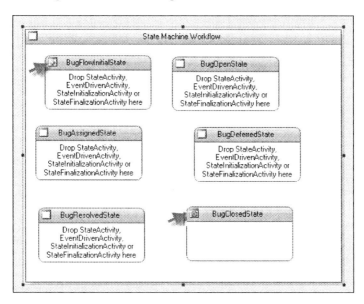

Notice two of the shapes in the screenshot above use special icons in their upper left corner. The BugFlowInitialState shape has a green icon in the upper left because it is the **initial state** for the workflow. Every state machine workflow must have an initial state, which the workflow will enter on start up. We can change the initial state by right-clicking another shape and selecting **Set As Initial State** from the context menu.

The BugClosedState has a red icon in the upper left because this is the **completed state**. A workflow is finished upon entering the completed state, but a completed state is optional. In many bug-tracking systems, a bug can be re-opened from a closed state, but in our workflow we will make the closed state a completed state. We can set the completed state by right-clicking a shape and selecting **Set As Completed State** from the context menu.

Our next step is to define the events the state machine will process in each state. We will define these events using an EventDriven activity.

The EventDriven Activity

The EventDriven activity is one of the few activities we can drag from the **Toolbox** and drop inside a State activity. In the screenshot below, we've dropped an EventDriven activity inside of BugFlowInitialState. We've also used the **Properties** window to change the EventDriven activity's name to OnBugOpened.

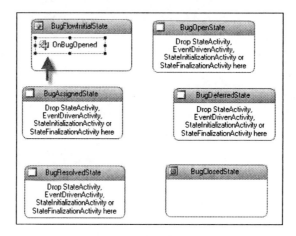

OnBugOpened represents how the state machine will react to a BugOpened event in its initial state. We cannot do much with the activity at this level of detail. We need to drill into the activity by double-clicking OnBugOpened. This brings us to the details view of the activity shown in the screenshot below:

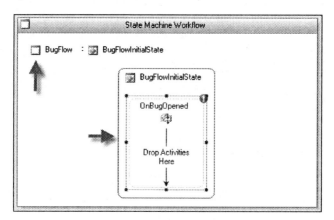

This detail view shows a *breadcrumb* navigation control along the top of the designer. The purpose of the breadcrumb is to let us know we are editing the BugFlowInitalState activity inside the BugFlow workflow. In the center of this view is a detailed view of the OnBugOpened EventDriven activity we dropped inside the state.

Inside the detailed view, we can see the EventDriven activity is like a sequence activity and can hold additional child activities. There are a few restrictions, however. The first activity in an EventDriven activity must implement the IEventActivity interface. Three activities from the base activity library meet this condition — the Delay activity, the HandleExternalEvent activity, and the WebServiceInput activity. All of our events will come from a local communication service, so we will use a HandleExternalEvent activity.

The screenshot below shows a HandleExternalEvent activity inside the OnBugOpened activity. We've changed the activity's name to handleBugOpenedEvent and set InterfaceType to reference the IBugService interface we defined earlier. Finally, we selected BugOpened as the name of the event to handle. We've done all the setup work we need to handle an event in our initial workflow state.

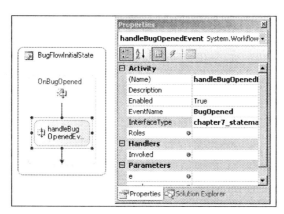

At this point, we could continue to add activities after the event handler. For example, we could add an activity to send notifications to team members about the new bug. When we are done adding these processing activities then the last activity we want to execute will be a SetState activity, which we cover next.

The SetState Activity

Incoming events force state machines to transition into new states. We can model transitions using the SetState activity, which can only appear inside state machine workflows. The SetState activity is relatively simple. The activity includes a TargetStateName property that points to the destination state.

In the following screenshot, we've added a `SetState` activity to `OnBugOpened` and set the `TargetStateName` property to `BugOpenState`. The property editor for `TargetStateName` will include only valid state names in a drop-down list for selection.

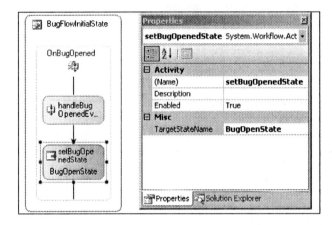

We can now click on the `BugFlow` link in the breadcrumb and return to view our state machine workflow. The designer will recognize the `SetState` activity we just configured and draw a line from the `BugFlowInitialState` shape to the `BugOpenState` (see screenshot below). The workflow designer gives us a clear picture that the workflow of a bug starts in `BugFlowInitialState`, and moves to the `BugOpenState` when an incoming `BugOpened` event signals the official birth of a new bug.

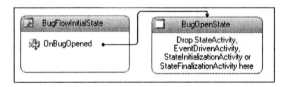

At this point, we can continue to add `EventDriven` activities to our workflow. We need to cover all the possible events and transitions in the life of a bug. One advantage of a state machine is that we control which events are legal in specific states. For example, we never want any state other than the initial state to handle a `BugOpened` event. We could also design our state machine so that a bug in the deferred state will only process a `BugAssigned` event. The following screenshot shows our state machine with all the events and transitions in place.

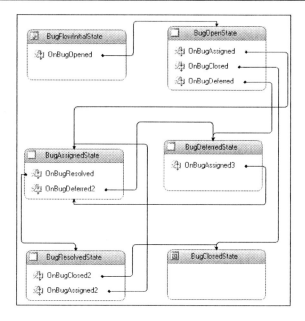

Notice in the screenshot above how the BugClosedState does not process any events. This state is the completed state, and the workflow will not process any additional events.

The StateInitialization and StateFinalization Activities

Two additional activities we can drop inside a State activity are the StateInitialization activity and the StateFinalization activity. A State activity can have only one StateInitialization activity and one StateFinalization activity.

Both of these activities will execute a set of child activities in sequence. The StateInitialization activity runs when the state machines transitions into the state containing the initialization activity. Conversely, the StateFinalization activity will execute whenever the state machine transitions out of the state containing the finalization activity. Using these two activities, we can perform pre- and post-processing inside the states of our state machines.

Driving the State Machine

Starting a state machine workflow is no different from starting any other workflow. We first create an instance of the WorkflowRuntime class. We will need the runtime to host an ExternalDataExchangeService, which in turn hosts our local

communication service that implements the `IBugService` interface. Chapter 3
covered local communication services and the `ExternalDataExchangeService` in
more detail.

```
ExternalDataExchangeService dataExchange;
dataExchange = new ExternalDataExchangeService();
workflowRuntime.AddService(dataExchange);

BugService bugService = new BugService();
dataExchange.AddService(bugService);

WorkflowInstance instance;
instance = workflowRuntime.CreateWorkflow(
                    typeof(BugFlow));
instance.Start();
```

The next bit of code in our program will invoke methods on our bug service. These
methods raise events that the workflow runtime will catch. We've carefully arranged
the events to move through all the states in the workflow and finish successfully.

```
Bug bug = new Bug();
bug.Title = "Application crash while printing";

bugService.OpenBug(instance.InstanceId, bug);
bugService.DeferBug(instance.InstanceId, bug);
bugService.AssignBug(instance.InstanceId, bug);
bugService.ResolveBug(instance.InstanceId, bug);
bugService.CloseBug(instance.InstanceId, bug);

waitHandle.WaitOne();
```

One of the advantages to using a state machine is that the workflow runtime will
raise an exception if our application fires an event that the current workflow state
doesn't expect. We should only fire the `BugOpened` event when the state machine is in
its initial state, and we should only fire the `BugResolved` event when the workflow
is in an assigned state. The workflow runtime will ensure our application follows the
process described by the state machine. This provides an advantage in that it ensures
an improperly coded application won't be able to cause state transitions that the
workflow does not regard as applicable, so the workflow-encoded business process
will always be followed. However, it's important to note that any code that fires
inapplicable events won't cause compile-time errors—we won't see the errors
until run time.

In a real bug-tracking application, it may take weeks or more for a bug to reach a
closed state. Fortunately, state machine workflows can take advantage of workflow
services, like tracking and persistence (both described in Chapter 6). A persistence
service could save the state of our workflow and unload the instance from memory,
then reload the instance when an event arrives weeks later.

There is something else unusual about our example. Our application knows the state of the workflow as it fires each event. A real application might not have this intimate knowledge of the workflow. Our application might not remember the state of a two-month-old bug, in which case it won't know the legal events to fire, either. Fortunately, Windows Workflow makes this information available.

Inspecting State Machines

Think about the user interface that we want to provide for our bug-tracking service. We wouldn't want to give the user the option to create exceptions. For instance, we wouldn't want to offer a **Close This Bug** button when the bug is in a state that will not transition to the closed state. Instead, we want the user interface to reflect the current state of the bug and only allow the user to perform legal actions. We can do this with the help of the StateMachineWorkflowInstance class.

StateMachineWorkflowInstance

The StateMachineWorkflowInstance class provides an API for us to manage and query a state machine workflow. As shown in the class diagram in the screenshot below, this API includes properties we can use to fetch the current state name and find the legal transitions for the state. The class also includes a method to set the state of the state machine. Although we generally want the bug to follow the workflow we've designed in our state machine, we could use the SetState method from an Administrator's override screen to put the bug back into its initial state, or to force the bug into a closed state (or any state in-between).

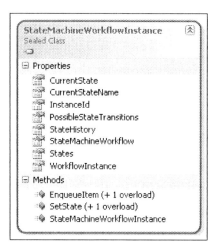

Let's modify our original example to call the following method. We will call this `DumpWorkflow` method just after calling the bug service's `AssignBug` method, so the workflow should be in the *Assigned* state.

```
private static void DumpStateMachine(
                    WorkflowRuntime runtime,
                    Guid instanceID)
{
    StateMachineWorkflowInstance instance =
            new StateMachineWorkflowInstance(
                runtime, instanceID);

    Console.WriteLine("Workflow ID: {0}", instanceID);
    Console.WriteLine("Current State: {0}",
                    instance.CurrentStateName);
    Console.WriteLine("Possible Transitions: {0}",
                    instance.PossibleStateTransitions.Count);
    foreach (string name in instance.PossibleStateTransitions)
    {
        Console.WriteLine("\t{0}", name);
    }
}
```

This code first retrieves a workflow instance object using the workflow runtime and a workflow ID. We then print out the name of the current state of the workflow, the number of legal transitions, and the names of the legal transitions. The output will look as shown below:

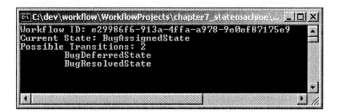

We can use the information above to customize the user interface. If the user were to open this particular bug in an application while the state of the bug was `BugAssignedState`, we'd provide buttons to mark the bug as resolved, or defer the bug. These are the only legal transitions from the current state.

Another interesting property on the `StateMachineWorkflowInstance` class is the `StateHistory` property. As you might imagine, this property can give us a list of all the states the workflow has seen. If you remember our discussion of tracking services from Chapter 6, you might remember the tracking service does a thorough job of recording the execution history of a workflow. If you guessed that the `StateHistory` property would use the built-in tracking service of WF, you guessed right!

State Machine Tracking

Chapter 6 provides all the details we needed to configure, initialize, and consume tracking and trace information, so we won't recover the same ground here. In order to make use of the `StateHistory` property, we have to configure the workflow runtime to use a tracking service. If we try to use the `StateHistory` property without a tracking service in place, we'll only create an `InvalidOperationException`.

StateHistory and the Tracking Service

As of this writing, the `StateHistory` property doesn't work if we configure the tracking service declaratively in `app.config` or `web.config`. Instead, we have to programmatically configure the tracking service with a connection string and pass the service to the workflow runtime:

```
SqlTrackingService trackingService;
trackingService = new SqlTrackingService(
            ConfigurationManager.
            ConnectionStrings["WorkflowDB"].
            ConnectionString);
trackingService.UseDefaultProfile = true;
workflowRuntime.AddService(trackingService);
```

If we want to list the states that our bug has passed through, we could use the classes we covered in Chapter 6, such as the `SqlTrackingQuery`. We can also use the `StateMachineWorkflowInstance` class and the `StateHistory` property to do all the work for us. Let's call the following method just before closing our bug:

```
private static void DumpHistory(
                    WorkflowRuntime runtime,
                    Guid instanceID)
{
    StateMachineWorkflowInstance instance =
            new StateMachineWorkflowInstance(
                    runtime, instanceID);

    Console.WriteLine("State History:");
    foreach (string name in instance.StateHistory)
    {
        Console.WriteLine("\t{0}", name);
    }
}
```

This code gives us the output as shown below: a list of the states the workflow has seen, starting with the most recently visited state.

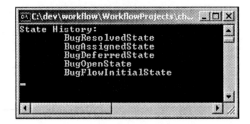

We can only use the `StateMachineWorkflowInstance` class while the workflow instance is still running. Once the workflow instance completes, we have to fall back to the tracking service and use tracking service queries to read the history of a state machine.

Hierarchical State Machines

Our first state machine was relatively simple, but it did represent the basic design for conventional state machines. Sometimes, however, this straightforward approach can be difficult to manage. Imagine if the workflow for our bug-tracking software required us to allow a user to close or assign a bug — regardless of the current state of the bug. We'd have to add event-driven activities for the assigned and closed events to *every* state in the workflow (except the completed state). This might be fine when we only have a handful of states, but can become tedious and error prone as the state machine grows.

Fortunately, there is an easier solution. A **hierarchical state machine** allows us to nest child states inside parent states. The child states essentially inherit the events driven activities of their parent. If every state in our bug tracking workflow needs to handle the bug-closed event with the same behavior, we only need to add one event-driven activity to a parent state, and add our bug states as children of this parent.

As it turns out, the state machine workflow itself is an instance of the `StateMachineWorkflowActivity` class, which derives from the `StateActivity` class (see the screenshot on the next page).

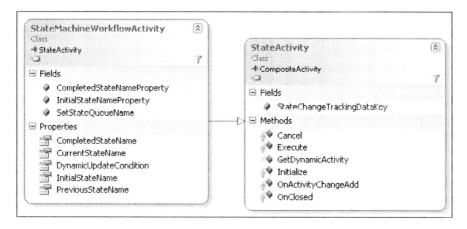

Given this bit of information, all we need to do is add event-driven activities for common events into our workflow, instead of inside each state. In the screenshot below, we've removed the event-driven activities for the bug assigned and bug-closed events from the individual states, and dropped them into the parent workflow.

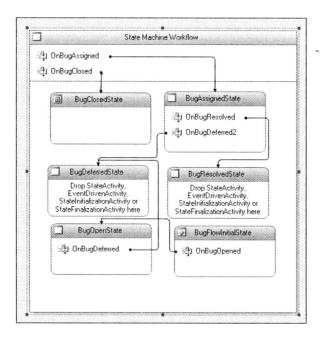

You'll notice this step has reduced the complexity of our state machine a bit. In fact, the BugDefferedState and BugResolvedState activities have no event-driven activities inside them at all. Instead, they'll inherit the behavior of the parent and process only the OnBugAssigned and OnBugDeferred events. All the other states will inherit these event-driven activities, too. Hierarchical state machines are a good fit for business exceptions, like when a customer cancels an order. If the customer cancels, we have to stop the workflow no matter the current state.

> With hierarchical state machines, it is important to realize that a SetState activity can only target a leaf state—that is a state with no child states.

Summary

In this chapter we've looked at state machines in Windows Workflow. State machines consist of states, events, and transitions. Windows Workflow provides all the activities we need to model these constituent pieces. State machines will typically be driven by a local communication service or web service requests, and the workflow runtime services, like tracking and persistence, work alongside state machines the same way they work with sequential workflows. Finally, hierarchical state machines enable us to extract common event-driven activities and place them into a parent state.

8

Communication in Workflows

Not many workflows will live in isolation. Most workflows will need to communicate with either local or remote services to finish their job. In earlier chapters, we've looked at some of the basic building blocks for communication in Windows Workflow. These blocks include activities like the `HandleExternalEvent` and `WebServiceInput` activities.

In this chapter, we drill into more details about communication in Windows Workflow. We'll see how a host process can communicate with specific activities inside a workflow, and also examine the underlying queuing mechanism that makes communication work. Finally, we look at remote communications using web services. By the end of this chapter, we'll have the knowledge required to build a well-connected application.

Local Communication Services Redux

We know that local communication services allow workflows to exchange data with their host process. In Chapter 3, we defined a service that raised a `BugAdded` event to a running workflow, which in turn invoked an `AssignBug` method on the service. The service sent data to the workflow via the event, and the workflow sent data to the service by invoking a method.

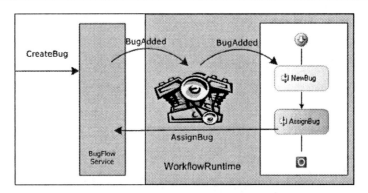

The screenshot above shows how the workflow runtime acts as a broker between the local communication service and a workflow instance. The runtime intercepts events from the local service and directs the events to the proper workflow instance. This interception is necessary because the workflow instance waiting for the event might have been unloaded from memory and persisted to a database table. The runtime can ask the persistence service to reload the workflow before it delivers an event, but it needs a workflow instance ID first. Even if the workflow is still in memory, the runtime will need an instance ID to locate the proper workflow. The runtime uses the instance ID required by the ExternalDataEventArgs object passed during the event.

In many ways, we can think of the instance ID as being like a street address on a package waiting for delivery. Given a street address, we can deliver the package to the correct building. If only one person lives at the address, we can be reasonably sure we've delivered the package to the intended recipient. But what if the street address leads us to an office building? We don't have enough information to correlate the package with its intended recipient.

Our simple example from Chapter 3 only has a single activity waiting for an event. The runtime doesn't require any additional information to deliver the payload. Not all workflows can be this simplistic. We'll need to learn how to correlate our messages in case there are multiple activities waiting for an event.

Correlation Parameters

Windows Workflow uses correlation tokens to establish conversations between specific activities inside a workflow and local communication services inside the host. Communication interfaces are uncorrelated by default; and we only need to establish these correlation tokens when a workflow has multiple activities waiting concurrently for incoming events. Let's look at an example:

Imagine we are developing a workflow for our bug-tracking application that will ask team members to vote on an incoming bug. A **yes** vote means the team member is willing to accept the bug into the system. A **no** vote means the team member wants to close the bug. We might design the interface and event argument class like the following:

```
[ExternalDataExchange]
public interface IBugVotingService
{
    void RequestVote(string userName);
    event EventHandler<VoteCompletedEventArgs> VoteCompleted;
}

[Serializable]
public class VoteCompletedEventArgs : ExternalDataEventArgs
{
    public VoteCompletedEventArgs(
                            Guid instanceId,
                            string userName,
                            bool isYesVote)
        : base(instanceId)
    {
        _userName = userName;
        _isYesVote = isYesVote;
    }

    private string _userName;
    public string UserName
    {
        get { return _userName; }
        set { _userName = value; }
    }

    private bool _isYesVote;
    public bool IsYesVote
    {
        get { return _isYesVote; }
        set { _isYesVote = value; }
    }
}
```

The workflow will invoke the RequestVote external method and pass a username as a parameter. It will be the service's responsibility to notify the user and wait to collect the user's vote. The service can then package the vote result into an event argument object and raise the VoteCompleted event. The workflow will receive the event, inspect the event arguments, and decide what to do next.

Now imagine a workflow like the one in screenshot below:

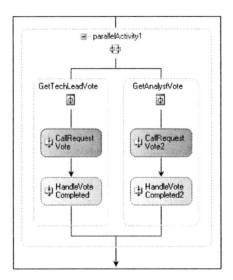

When we designed our service interface, we assumed a workflow would only go looking for a single vote. The workflow in the screenshot above is looking for two votes in parallel. The workflow will call the service asking for a vote from the team's technical lead. The workflow will also call the service asking for a vote from the team's analyst. It will then wait for both events to arrive before it completes the parallel activity.

 Remember the `ParallelActivity`, which we covered in Chapter 4, doesn't offer true parallel processing. The runtime only allows one thread to execute inside a workflow instance at a time. The parallel activity here will use that one thread to execute both branches in no deterministic order, until they block and wait for an event. Since it is unlikely that one of voting team members will respond with a vote in milliseconds, both branches of the parallel activity will reach a state where they are blocked and waiting for their respective events to arrive.

Suppose the team's technical lead is the first to respond with a vote. The service will raise an event, which the workflow runtime will intercept. The runtime will then find our workflow instance and deliver the event. The question is — will the runtime deliver the technical lead's vote to the `HandleExternalEvent` activity waiting in the left branch, or the right branch? We can't be certain. The tech lead's vote might end up in the right side, which we designed to process the analyst's vote. This scenario presents a problem we have to solve by giving the runtime more information.

Correlation Attributes

When the workflow calls out to the RequestVote method, it includes a significant piece of information—the username parameter. If we ask for a vote from **scott,** we should get Scott's vote back in the following activity. The username parameter can tie the activities together—we just need to inform the workflow of the parameter's significance. The following code is a revised version of our service's interface, along with the event argument class:

```
[ExternalDataExchange]
[CorrelationParameter("userName")]
public interface IBugVotingService
{
    [CorrelationAlias("userName", "e.UserName")]
    event EventHandler<VoteCompletedEventArgs> VoteCompleted;

    [CorrelationInitializer]
    void RequestVote(string userName);
}

[Serializable]
public class VoteCompletedEventArgs : ExternalDataEventArgs
{
    public VoteCompletedEventArgs(
                            Guid instanceId,
                            string userName,
                            bool isYesVote)
        : base(instanceId)
    {
        _userName = userName;
        _isYesVote = isYesVote;
    }

    private string _userName;
    public string UserName
    {
        get { return _userName; }
        set { _userName = value; }
    }

    private bool _isYesVote;
    public bool IsYesVote
    {
        get { return _isYesVote; }
        set { _isYesVote = value; }
    }
}
```

We have three new attributes on our service interface. These attributes contain correlation metadata that the runtime can use to set up a conversation between our service and individual activities inside a workflow.

Correlation Parameter

We've added a `CorrelationParameter` attribute to our interface. The attribute specifies the name of a parameter that the runtime will use to map an event to a specific `HandleExternalEvent` activity. We specified `userName` as our correlation parameter. The runtime will look for a parameter with the name of `userName` on all methods and events in the communication service interface. When it finds such a parameter it will use the parameter for correlation.

The `CorrelationParameter` attribute can appear multiple times on an interface if there are multiple correlation parameters. We can only use this attribute on interface types.

Correlation Initializer

We've decorated the `RequestVote` method with a `CorrelationInitializer` attribute. The workflow runtime will recognize a call to `RequestVote` as the start of a conversation between the workflow and the communication service. The runtime will also recognize the username parameter as the correlation parameter, and save the value. Later, when events arrive for the workflow, the runtime will compare incoming correlation parameters against the saved values.

The obvious question is—how does the workflow know what the correlation parameter is for an event? There is no username parameter—we've encapsulated the username *inside* the event arguments. This is where the third attribute steps in—the `CorrelationAlias` attribute.

Correlation Alias

We can apply `CorrelationAlias` attributes to methods and events in our service interface to override the `CorrelationParameter` attribute on individual members. We've placed this attribute on the `VoteCompleted` event. The attribute tells the runtime to fetch the username correlation parameter from the `UserName` property of the e parameter.

We've set up all the metadata we need in our service interface. The workflow runtime will have enough information to correlate a `CallExternalMethod` activity passing a username of **scott** with a `HandleExternalEvent` activity waiting on the vote result for **scott**. Our next step is to utilize the correlation metadata inside our workflow.

Correlation Tokens

When we drop a `CallExternalMethod` activity into the workflow designer, we have to configure, at a minimum, the `InterfaceType` and `MethodName` properties. These properties tell WF the service and service method we want the activity to invoke. If the interface we configure has a `CorrelationParameter` attribute, the designer will add a new property to the **Properties** window—a `CorrelationToken` property (see screenshot below).

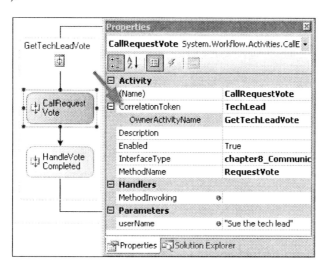

Windows Workflow uses correlation tokens to link activities in a conversation. We need to give the token a name and an owner. The token name is arbitrary, but since it does identify the token, we should choose a meaningful name. The owner must be an ancestor of the current activity. In the screenshot above, we've named the correlation token **TechLead** and assigned its parent, the parallel activity branch, as the owner of the token.

The `HandleExternalEvent` activity is next in this branch, and this activity should handle the tech lead's vote. Once we've assigned the `InterfaceType` and `EventName` properties in this activity, we'll again see a `CorrelationToken` property appear. We will want to select `TechLead` in the token's drop-down list.

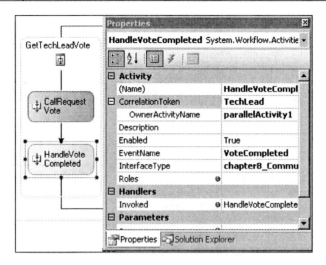

We've linked the `CallExternalMethod` activity and `HandleExternalEvent` activity in the left branch with a correlation token. We can also create a new token for the pair of activities in the right branch. The workflow runtime will use these tokens and the username parameter to make sure it delivers the votes to the proper event handler.

While correlation tokens are useful for linking activities, we shouldn't depend upon them as a security feature. Just because a vote says it is from the technical lead doesn't mean the message is *really* from the technical lead. In the next section, we will learn how to use another property of the `HandleExternalEvent` activity — the `Roles` property.

Role-Based Authorization

Protecting computer resources is a two-step process. The first step is authentication. Authentication verifies a user's identity. Authentication might be as simple as asking a person for their username and password, or might be more involved and utilize biometric information, like a fingerprint or retina scan. Windows Workflow doesn't authenticate users, but when authentication is required the runtime will rely on authentication mechanisms in the software around it. For instance, a workflow hosted inside of an ASP.NET application might need Integrated Windows authentication enabled, or might rely on the ASP.NET membership provider to authenticate users.

Once a user's identity is established, we can determine what actions we will allow the user to perform. This is step two — authorization. Authorization rules often sound like **only managers can approve an expense account** or **only administrators can cancel the operation**. Notice that these rules refer to groups of users like managers and administrators. This is because we typically assign roles to our users and authorize their requests based on their roles (hence the term — role-based authorization).

In the software world, role management software comes in a variety of flavors. For software inside a Windows domain, we might derive a user's roles from their Active Directory group membership. In a public-facing ASP.NET web application, we might derive a user's roles from the ASP.NET Role Provider.

To support the different role implementations, Windows Workflow provides an extensible role management scheme. WF provides an abstract base class named `WorkflowRole`. The built-in implementations of this class provide role management for Windows Active Directory and ASP.NET 2.0 Role Providers:

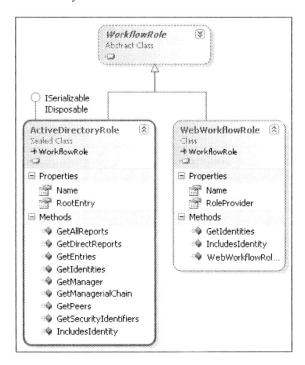

Roles and Activities

The two WF activities providing support for role-based authorization are the `HandleExternalEvent` activity and the `WebServiceInput` activity. Both expose a `Roles` property that is of type `WorkflowRoleCollection`. If we want to use role-based authorization to secure these activities, we'll need to bind the `Roles` property to a valid collection. In the following code we've declared a public field with the name of `validRoles`. In the workflow `Initialized` event handler, we add a single new `WebWorkflowRole` instance to the `validRoles` collection.

```
public partial class BugFlowWithRoles : SequentialWorkflowActivity
{
    public WorkflowRoleCollection validRoles =
                new WorkflowRoleCollection();

    private void BugFlowWithRoles_Initialized(object sender,
                                                EventArgs e)
    {
        validRoles.Add(new WebWorkflowRole("TechLeads"));
    }
}
```

With our roles in place, we need to configure our activities to utilize the roles.

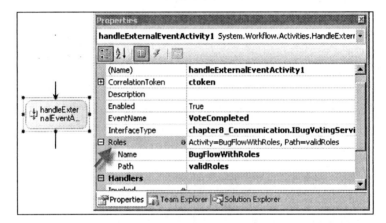

When a local communication service host raises an event for the workflow, it can pass along a Windows identity parameter in the `ExternalDataEventArgs` object's `Identity` property. The activity will compare the roles assigned to the identity to the roles in the `Roles` collection. If there is a match, the activity will continue execution. If there is no match the activity will throw a `WorkflowAuthorizationException`. We could manage this exception with a fault handler in our workflow, or let the exception terminate the workflow. Note that if the local communication service does not explicitly pass an identity in the event arguments, the workflow runtime will use the identity associated with the current thread.

When we use the `CallExternalMethod` and `HandleExternalEvent` activities to communicate with a host, we are working at a relatively high level of abstraction. The built-in features like role-based authorization and correlation take away many of the headaches associated with messaging systems. However, there can come a time when a design requires the additional flexibility that comes from working closer to the metal. In the next section, we'll look at the queuing mechanism that lives underneath these high-level communication activities.

Workflow Queues

If you think back to the diagram at the beginning of this chapter, you'll remember our conversation about the workflow runtime intercepting events. It's the runtime's responsibility to deliver an event to the proper activity inside a specific workflow instance. But how does the runtime deliver an event? The runtime can't just raise the event on an arbitrary thread — only one thread can execute inside an instance at a time.

The answer is a queuing service that is part of the workflow runtime. Activities use this service to create queues that can hold incoming data. An activity can then subscribe for a notification when an item arrives in the queue. These queues become part of the workflow and are serialized with the workflow when the persistence service serializes and saves a workflow instance. This is one reason why our data-exchange event arguments are marked as serializable.

When the runtime delivers an event to a workflow, it picks the correct queue for the event, and adds the event arguments to the queue. Each queue exposes information that will allow the runtime to match up types and correlation parameters when selecting the correct queue. At the bottom of the screenshot overleaf, we've hinted that the runtime will use the workflow queue name to route the event. We'll see details about the queue name in the next section.

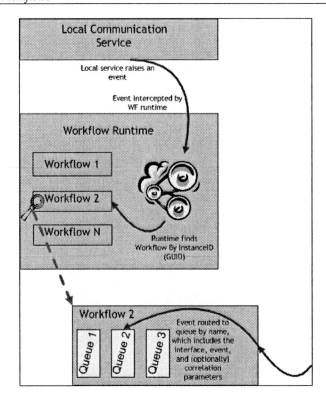

WorkflowQueue and WorkflowQueueInfo

The screenshot on the page opposite shows the WorkflowQueue class, which represents a queue inside a workflow instance, and the WorkflowQueueInfo class, which can describe a queue. Typically, when we use event listening activities like HandleExternalEvent or Delay activities, we don't need to know about these underlying queues. However, these queues can enable a number of scenarios that are impossible at the higher level of abstraction. Let's take a look at some examples.

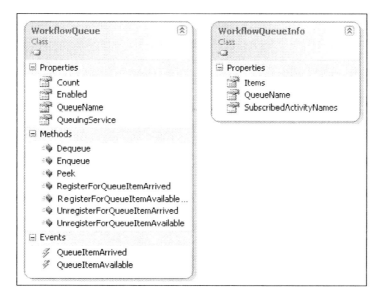

Finding the Waiting Activity

Let's return to our workflow from the beginning of the chapter. Inside the workflow we used HandleExternalEvent activities inside two branches of a Parallel activity. These event handlers wait for vote events to arrive from the local communication service, and use correlation tokens to ensure the vote arrives in the correct branch. We will call the following code inside an event handler for the runtime's WorkflowIdled event. The runtime fires this event when the workflow is blocked and waiting for events to arrive.

```
static void DumpQueueInfo(WorkflowInstance workflow)
{
    ReadOnlyCollection<WorkflowQueueInfo> queueInfos;
    queueInfos = workflow.GetWorkflowQueueData();

    Console.WriteLine("Queue Info for {0}",
                      workflow.InstanceId);

    for (int i = 0; i < queueInfos.Count; i++)
    {
        Console.WriteLine();
        Console.WriteLine("Queue #{0}", i.ToString());
        Console.WriteLine(queueInfos[i].QueueName);
        Console.Write("Subscribed activities: ");

        ReadOnlyCollection<string> names =
            queueInfos[i].SubscribedActivityNames;
```

```
        foreach (string name in names)
        {
            Console.Write("{0} ", name);
        }
        Console.WriteLine();
        Console.WriteLine();
    }
}
```

For each queue in the workflow instance, we will print out the queue's name and a list of subscribed activities. The output will look as shown below:

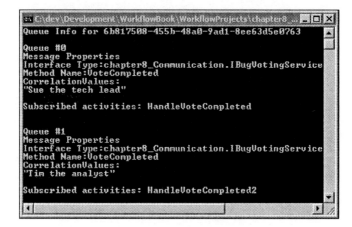

From this output, we can see there are two queues in our workflow instance. Where we printed the queue name we see **Message Properties** output. It turns out the name of these queues described the types of events they are waiting for. Remember, queue names in a workflow instance must be unique for the runtime to deliver an event to the correct queue. Both queues contain the same **Interface Type** and **Method Name** (event name) in their respective names. Fortunately, the **Correlation Values**, which are also part of the queue name, are different. These correlation values are the values of the `userName` parameters that we passed to the service method with the `CorrelationInitializer` attribute present (`RequestVote`).

If we want to work with queue names for the `HandleExternalEvent` activity in a strongly typed manner, we can cast the queue name to an instance of the `EventQueueName` class. The class provides `InterfaceType` and `MethodName` properties to break the queue name into its constituent parts. There is also a method (`GetCorrelationValues`) to inspect the correlation values.

It should now be obvious that when the workflow runtime needs to deliver an event to a workflow activity, it doesn't go looking for a specific activity, but for a specific queue. The runtime can compare the incoming event information (interface, name, and correlation values) to these queue names to find the proper queue for the event. The activity only needs to wait for events to arrive in the queue.

From the output in the screenshot below, we can also deduce which activities are waiting for events. These activities will appear in the list of subscribed activities. Let's say the analyst votes immediately, and our workflow returns to an idle state to wait for the tech lead to vote. Our queue dump will look as shown below:

Now we are down to a single blocking activity. Our application could use this type of queue information to troubleshoot or assist with blocked workflows (we could also use tracking information).

Canceling a Waiting Activity

What happens if we just want to cancel a waiting activity? Perhaps the vote will not be forthcoming because our company fired all the technical staff. This is another scenario where queue operations are useful.

The `WorkflowInstance` class offers an `EnqueueItem` method. Given a queue name and an object, the `EnqueueItem` method will place the object into the queue of the given name. If we place an exception object in the queue, we can cancel a `HandleExternalEvent` activity with an error:

```
ReadOnlyCollection<WorkflowQueueInfo> queueInfos;
queueInfos = workflowInstance.GetWorkflowQueueData();

foreach (WorkflowQueueInfo queueInfo in queueInfos)
{
    workflowInstance.EnqueueItem(
        queueInfo.QueueName,
        new Exception(),
        null,
```

```
          null
     );
}
```

The workflow response to this exception will depend on the design of the workflow. If the workflow has a fault handler in scope, the new exception will bubble up to the fault handler. If there is no fault handler in scope, the exception will lead to a workflow termination.

Communicating with Queues

Workflow queues are for all forms of inbound communications. When we are using `HandleExternalEvent` and `Delay` activities, these queues are in play even when we don't interact with them directly. This higher level of abstraction comes at the cost of defining and adhering to formal communication interfaces.

There may be workflows that require more flexibility in their communication scenarios. In these cases we can create queues, perhaps from our own custom activities, that can receive data directly from the host process. The cost of this flexibility is the additional code required to manage and maintain our custom queues.

Web Service Communication

Not all communications will be local communications. Windows Workflow provides web service interoperability as an additional feature. WF allows us to expose a workflow as a web service, and consume a web service from a workflow.

Workflows as Web Services

In this section, we'll build a workflow to deploy as a web service. Our starting project will be a sequential workflow library. A library is ideally suited for hosting in an ASP.NET web application. We can rename `Workflow1.cs` in the new project to **HelloWorldWorkflow**.

Just like local communication services, web services require a contract that defines the members of a web service. The contract is an interface, but without all the data exchange attributes we've used in previous communication interfaces. The interface for our `HelloWorld` workflow is shown below:

```
interface IHelloWorldService
{
    string GetHelloWorldMessage(string name);
}
```

WebServiceInput Activity

The first activity for a web service workflow will be a `WebServiceInput` activity. The `WebServiceInput` activity represents a method in our web service contract that receives data from a web service request. Dropping a `WebServiceInput` activity into the designer and configuring the activity is somewhat similar to dropping and configuring a `HandleExternalEvent` activity. We need to set the `InterfaceType` and `MethodName` properties. Our `IHelloWorldService` interface only defines a single method: `GetHelloWorldMessage`. To implement this method we only need to configure a `WebServiceInput` activity as we have in the screenshot below:

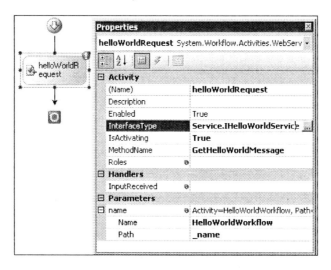

Another important property in a `WebServiceInput` activity is the `IsActivating` property. This property tells the workflow runtime that invoking the `GetHelloWorldMessage` web method will start execution of our workflow. We can have multiple `WebServiceInput` activities inside a workflow when we expect to see a sequence of web service calls to complete the workflow. Only the first input activity should have the `IsActivating` property set to true.

The workflow designer will examine the web service method we are implementing to uncover input parameters. The designer will make input parameters available for binding in the **Properties** windows. In the screenshot above we are using a binding to place the incoming name parameter into a _name field in our workflow.

Notice we still have a validation error in our input activity (there is a red exclamation point in the upper right of the shape). A `WebServiceInput` activity is not complete until we couple the activity with a `WebServiceOutput` activity.

WebServiceOutput Activity

A `WebServiceOutput` activity returns a response to web service clients. The `InputActivityName` is a required property on this activity. In the screenshot below we've dropped an output activity as the second activity in our workflow, and configured the `InputActivityName` with the name of our input activity. Both activities will now pass validation.

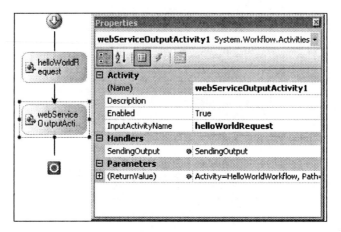

 A `WebServiceFault` activity exists to model exceptions in web services. The activity will return a SOAP exception to the client. We do not have a `WebServiceFault` in this workflow.

In the screenshot above we've also configured a `SendingOutput` event handler, and bound the return value (the output of our web service) to a `_result` field in our workflow class. The entire listing of the workflow class appears below. In the `SendingOutput` event handler we build a response for the client and place the result in the `_result` field.

```
public sealed partial class HelloWorldWorkflow :
        SequentialWorkflowActivity
{
    public HelloWorldWorkflow()
    {
        InitializeComponent();
    }

    public string _name = String.Empty;
    public string _result;

    private void SendingOutput(object sender, EventArgs e)
```

```
    {
        _result = String.Format(
                "Hello World! Hello, {0}!",
                _name);
    }
}
```

Once we are sure the workflow compiles, we can move to make the service available for testing by publishing the web service.

Publishing Web Service Workflows

Publishing a workflow as a web service is a relatively simple operation. We need to right-click our workflow project and select **Publish as Web Service**. This action will kick off a series of steps inside Visual Studio. Visual Studio will create a new web service project, and add the project to our solution. The new project will have the name of our project followed by **_WebService**.

The new project will only contain a few files, and a reference to our workflow project. One file will be an asmx file, where asmx is the common extension for an ASP.NET web service endpoint. The generated contents of this file will look like the following:

```
<%@ WebService
   Class="Chapter8_WebService.HelloWorldWorkflow_WebService"
%>
```

The above is all the code necessary to wire up a workflow as a web service endpoint. The generated project will also include a web.config file. A portion of the configuration is shown below. Note that some type namespaces have been removed to allow the code to fit on a page.

```
<section
    name="WorkflowRuntime"
    type="WorkflowRuntimeSection,
         System.Workflow.Runtime,
         Version=3.0.00000.0, Culture=neutral,
         PublicKeyToken=31bf3856ad364e35"/>
</configSections>
<WorkflowRuntime Name="WorkflowServiceContainer">
    <Services>
      <add
         type="ManualWorkflowSchedulerService,
              System.Workflow.Runtime,
              Version=3.0.0.0, Culture=neutral,
```

```
                    PublicKeyToken=31bf3856ad364e35"/>
          <add
            type="DefaultWorkflowCommitWorkBatchService,
                System.Workflow.Runtime,
                Version=3.0.0.0, Culture=neutral,
                PublicKeyToken=31bf3856ad364e35"/>
        </Services>
    </WorkflowRuntime>
<system.web>
    <httpModules>
        <add
          type="WorkflowWebHostingModule,
                System.Workflow.Runtime,
                Version=3.0.0.0, Culture=neutral,
                PublicKeyToken=31bf3856ad364e35"
          name="WorkflowHost"/>
    </httpModules>
</system.web>
```

Notice the `web.config` replaces the default workflow scheduler with the manual workflow scheduler. We covered these services in Chapter 6. The manual workflow scheduler is the preferred scheduler in an ASP.NET scenario because it can execute the workflows synchronously on the same thread as the incoming web request.

The `WorkflowWebHostingModule` enables routing a client to an existing workflow instance using client-side cookies. In our scenario, the workflow instance will not need to span multiple web requests, so this service won't be utilized.

We can now right-click the `asmx` file and select **View In Browser** from the context menu. The ASP.NET web development web server will host the web service. We should see a browser page appear with a link to **GetHelloWorldMessage**. If we follow the link we'll see the screen as shown in the screenshot on the next page, which presents an opportunity to manually test the method.

The ASP.NET web development web server (WebDev) will pick a random port for serving up content and web services. This is a fine strategy for testing websites for development, but can make it difficult to reference the web service from another .NET project (because the port number can change between sessions). For best results, create a new virtual directory in IIS and map the virtual directory to the web service project's root. Another option is to choose a specific port with the WebDev server by going into the web project properties and setting **use dynamic port** to false, and selecting a port number.

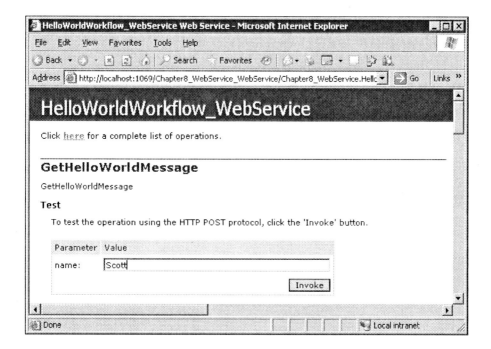

Filling in a name and clicking invoke should successfully execute our workflow. The result is shown overleaf.

Our web service is ready for consumption. In the next section, we will build a
workflow to call this web service.

Workflows as Web Service Clients

To consume the web service we built, we can return to our previous project, or
create a new console-mode workflow application. Any project can consume a
web service, even other class library projects and web service application projects.
In the screenshot below, we are adding a new **Sequential Workflow (with code
separation)** to our project named `HelloWorldClient`.

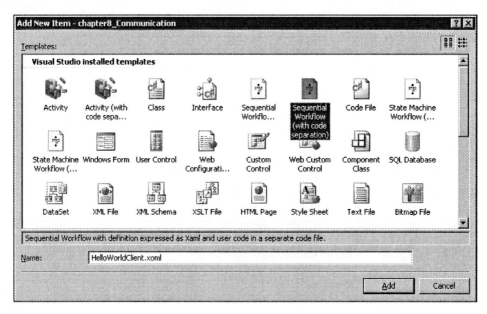

InvokeWebService Activity

As soon as the workflow designer opens, we can drag-and-drop an
`InvokeWebService` activity into the workflow. The designer will open a dialog box
asking us to create a web reference. We can enter the URL to the web service we
created earlier in the URL text box. Alternatively, if the web service is in the same
solution, we can click on the **Web Services** in this solution link in the dialog box.
Once the dialog box locates the web service, the display will change as shown below:

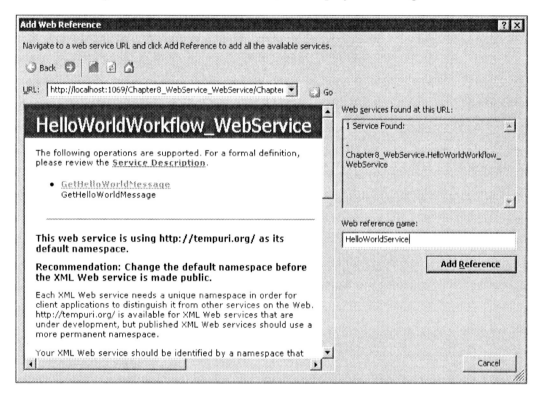

You can see that we've changed the web reference name to **HelloWorldService**. This
value sets the name of the web service proxy class that Visual Studio generates on
our behalf. It is through the proxy that we will invoke the web service. Clicking the
Add Reference button will add the proxy to our project.

Returning to the designer, we can now configure our `InvokeWebService` activity
(see the screenshot overleaf). The `ProxyClass` property is a drop-down list
containing all the web reference proxy classes in the project. In the screenshot, we've
selected a proxy and selected the `MethodName` from a drop-down list. We have also
configured our parameters, and bound an event handler.

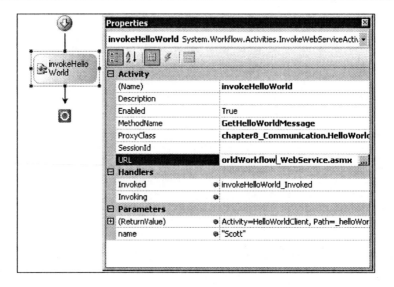

The code-behind for our workflow looks like the following:

```
public partial class HelloWorldClient :
        SequentialWorkflowActivity
{
    public string _helloWorldResult;

    private void invokeHelloWorld_Invoked(
                    object sender,
                    InvokeWebServiceEventArgs e)
    {
        Console.WriteLine("Hello world returned " +
                    _helloWorldResult);
    }
}
```

Running this workflow will result in a SOAP web service call to our last workflow.

Summary

In this chapter we've delved into the communication capabilities of Windows Workflow. We've seen how correlation attributes and correlation tokens can tie together related activities, and examined role-based authorization. Underneath the event-driven activities we've seen how workflow queues manage events and data arriving at the workflow. We can use these queues for our own communication purposes, or query the queues to see which activities are waiting for events inside a workflow. Finally, we examined the web service capabilities of Windows Workflow by building a simple web service, and a client to consume the web service.

9

Rules and Conditions

Software applies knowledge to data. This is true for all software from business applications to video games. The knowledge inside software is generally a combination of procedural knowledge and declarative knowledge. Procedural knowledge is information about *how* to perform a task, like how to make a car and hotel reservation using an electronic travel broker. Procedural knowledge is easy to express using a general-purpose programming language like C#, Visual Basic, or any of their predecessors.

Declarative knowledge, on the other hand, is about the relationships in data. We often refer to declarative knowledge as business rules. For example, a business rule might say that hotel reservations made at least 14 days in advance receive a 10% discount, unless the cost of the room is less than $100. The date and the price share a relationship and can affect each other. Expressing this type of knowledge using a general-purpose programming language isn't difficult on a small scale, but breaks down as the amount of knowledge grows. We must transform the knowledge into procedural code using if-then-else statements. Many software applications require an enormous number of business rules: tax preparation systems, mortgage-banking software, and hotel reservation systems, to name just a few.

Encoding business rules into procedural code makes the rules harder to find, read, and modify. Over the years, the software industry has invented tools for working with business rules. We categorize these tools as rules engines. A rules engine specializes in making declarative knowledge easier to implement, process, isolate, and modify.

Windows Workflow provides a rules engine and offers the best of both worlds. We can use `Sequence` activities to implement procedural knowledge, and `Policy` activities to execute declarative knowledge.

In this chapter, we will focus on the activities that use rules and conditions for declarative knowledge. We will start by looking at activities that use conditions, like the `While` activity. We will also discuss the `Policy` activity, which is a rules engine, and the `ConditionedActivityGroup`, which conditionally executes activities based on `When` and `Until` conditions.

What are Rules and Conditions?

Three important concepts we will use in this chapter are conditions, rules, and rule sets. In WF, **conditions** are chunks of logic that return true or false. A number of WF activities utilize conditions to guide their behavior. These activities include the `While` activity, the `IfElseBranch` activity, and the `ConditionedActivityGroup`. The `While` activity, for instance, loops until its `Condition` property returns false. We can implement conditions in code or in XML.

Rules are conditions with a set of actions to perform. Rules use a declarative if-then-else style, where the `if` is a condition to evaluate. If the condition evaluates to true, the runtime performs the `then` actions, otherwise the `else` actions. While this sounds like procedural code, there are substantial differences. The if-then-else constructs in most languages actively change the flow of control in an application. Rules, on the other hand, passively wait for an execution engine to evaluate their logic.

A **rule set** is a collection of one or more rules. As another example from the hotel business, we might have three rules we use to calculate the discount on the price of a room (shown here in pseudo-code).

```
if person's age is greater than 55
   then discount = discount + 10%

if length of stay is greater than 5 days
   then discount = discount + 10%

if discount is greater than 12%
   then discount = 12%
```

Before we can evaluate these rules, we need to group them inside a rule set. A rule set allows us to assign priorities to each rule and control their order of evaluation. WF can revisit rules if later rules change the data used inside previous rules. We can store rules in an external XML file and pass the rules to the workflow runtime when creating a new workflow. WF provides an API for us to programmatically update, create, and modify rule sets and rules at run time. The features and execution semantics described above give us more flexibility and control compared to compiled code. For instance, the APIs allow us to dynamically customize rules to meet the needs of a specific customer or business scenario.

We will return to rules and rule sets later in the chapter. For now we will drill into conditions in Windows Workflow.

Working with Conditions

The `While` activity is one activity that uses a condition. The `While` activity will repeatedly execute its child activity until its `Condition` property returns false. The **Properties** window for the `While` activity allows us to set this `Condition` property to a **Code Condition** or a **Declarative Rule Condition**. In the screenshot below, we've told the `While` activity to use a code condition, and that the code condition is implemented in a method named `CheckBugIndex`.

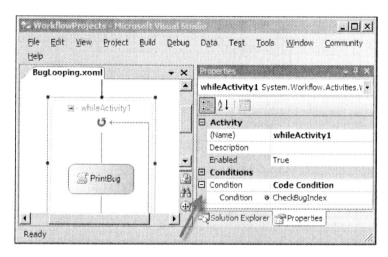

Code Conditions

A code condition is an event handler in our code-beside file. A code condition returns a boolean value via a `ConditionalEventArgs` parameter. Because a code condition is just another method on our workflow class, the conditional logic compiles into the same assembly that hosts our workflow definition.

The implementation of `CheckBugIndex` is shown below. We have an array of bug objects for the workflow to process. The array might arrive as a parameter to the workflow, or through some other communication mechanism like the `HandleExternalEvent` activity. The workflow uses the `bugIndex` field to track its progress through the array. Somewhere, another activity will increment `bugIndex` as the workflow finishes processing each bug. If the array of bugs is not initialized, or if the `bugIndex` doesn't point to a valid entry in the array, we want to halt the `While` activity by having our code condition return a value of false.

```
private Bug[] bugs;
private int bugIndex = 0;

protected void CheckBugIndex(object sender, ConditionalEventArgs e)
{
```

```
if (bugs == null || bugIndex >= bugs.Length)
{
  e.Result = false;
}
else
{
  e.Result = true;
}
}
```

Code conditions, like our method above, are represented by `CodeCondition` objects at run time. The `CodeCondition` class derives from an abstract `ActivityCondition` class (see the screenshot below).

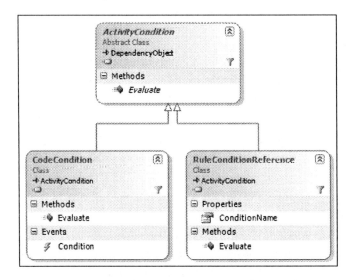

Because the `Condition` property of the `While` activity accepts an `ActivityCondition` object, we have the choice of assigning either a `CodeCondition` or a `RuleConditionReference`. Regardless of which type we choose, all the runtime needs to do is call the `Evaluate` method to fetch a Boolean result. A `CodeCondition` will ultimately fire its `Condition` event to retrieve this Boolean value. It is this `Condition` event that we are wiring up to the method in our code-behind file. We can see this a little more clearly by looking at the XAML markup produced by the designer.

```
<WhileActivity x:Name="whileActivity1">
  <WhileActivity.Condition>
    <CodeCondition Condition="CheckBugIndex" />
  </WhileActivity.Condition>
  <!-- child activity goes here-->
</WhileActivity>
```

We will see how a `RuleConditionReference` works in the next section.

Rule Conditions

Declarative rule conditions work differently from code conditions. If we expressed our `CheckBugIndex` condition as a declarative rule, we would just need to type the following string into the rule condition designer:

```
bugs == null || bugIndex >= bugs.Length
```

Windows Workflow will parse and evaluate this rule at run time. We don't need to create a new method in our workflow class. The definition for this expression will ultimately live inside a `.rules` file as part of our workflow project. A `RuleConditionReference` object will reference the expression by name, as every rule in WF has a name.

As an example, suppose we are creating a new workflow with a `While` activity, and we want the activity to loop until a `_retryCount` field exceeds some value. After we drop the `While` activity in the designer, we can open the **Properties** windows and click the drop-drown list beside the `Condition` property. This time, we will ask for a **Declarative Rule Condition**. The designer will make two additional entries available—**ConditionName** and **Expression**. Clicking in the text box beside **ConditionName** will display the ellipsis pointed to in screenshot below:

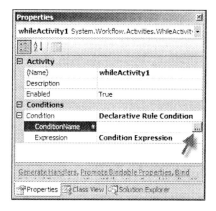

Clicking the ellipsis button launches the **Select Condition** dialog box, shown in the following screenshot. This dialog box will list all of the declarative rule conditions in our workflow, and will initially be empty. Along the top of the dialog box are buttons to create, edit, rename, and delete rules. The **Valid** column on the right-hand side will let us know about syntax errors and other validation problems in our rules. When we select a condition, the **Condition Preview** area will show us the code for the condition.

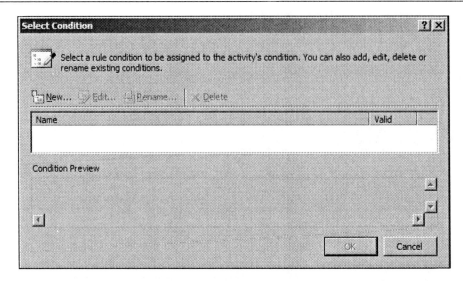

At this point we want to create a new rule. Clicking the **New...** button will launch the **Rule Condition Editor** dialog box as shown below:

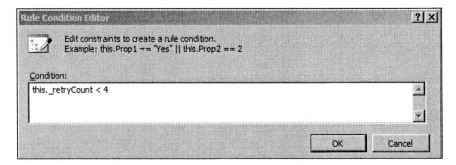

Inside this editor is where we can type our expression. The expression we've entered will return true as long as the _retryCount field is less than 4. If we type the C# this keyword (or the Me keyword in Visual Basic), an IntelliSense window will appear and display a list of fields, properties, and methods in our workflow class.

Clicking the **OK** button in the editor will return us to the **Select Condition** dialog box, where we can click the **Rename** button to give our condition a friendly name (the default name would be **Condition1**, which isn't descriptive). We will give our rule the name of RetryCountCondition.

The .rules File

After all these button clicks, a new file will appear nested underneath our workflow definition in the **Solution Explorer** window. The file will have the same name as our workflow class name but with an extension of `.rules`. Inside is a verbose XML representation of the condition we wrote.

```
<RuleDefinitions
  xmlns="http://schemas.microsoft.com/winfx/2006/xaml/workflow">
  <RuleDefinitions.Conditions>
    <RuleExpressionCondition Name="RetryCountCondition">
      <RuleExpressionCondition.Expression>
        <ns0:CodeBinaryOperatorExpression Operator="LessThan"
          xmlns:ns0="clr-namespace:System.CodeDom;
                    Assembly=System, Version=2.0.0.0,
                    Culture=neutral,
                    PublicKeyToken=b77a5c561934e089">
        <ns0:CodeBinaryOperatorExpression.Left>
          <ns0:CodeFieldReferenceExpression
              FieldName="_retryCount">
            <ns0:CodeFieldReferenceExpression.TargetObject>
              <ns0:CodeThisReferenceExpression />
            </ns0:CodeFieldReferenceExpression.TargetObject>
          </ns0:CodeFieldReferenceExpression>
        </ns0:CodeBinaryOperatorExpression.Left>
        <ns0:CodeBinaryOperatorExpression.Right>
          <ns0:CodePrimitiveExpression>
            <ns0:CodePrimitiveExpression.Value>
              <ns1:Int32
                xmlns:ns1="clr-namespace:System;
                  Assembly=mscorlib, Version=2.0.0.0,
                  Culture=neutral, PublicKeyToken=b77a5c561934e089"
                >
                4
              </ns1:Int32>
            </ns0:CodePrimitiveExpression.Value>
          </ns0:CodePrimitiveExpression>
        </ns0:CodeBinaryOperatorExpression.Right>
      </ns0:CodeBinaryOperatorExpression>
      </RuleExpressionCondition.Expression>
    </RuleExpressionCondition>
  </RuleDefinitions.Conditions>
</RuleDefinitions>
```

If you remember our XAML discussion from Chapter 2, you'll realize this is a XAML representation of objects from the `System.CodeDom` namespace. The `CodeDom` (Code Document Object Model) namespace contains classes that construct source code in a language-agnostic fashion. For instance, the `CodeBinaryOperatorExpression` class represents a binary operator between two expressions. The instance in our XAML is a `LessThan` operator, but could be an addition, subtraction, greater than, or bitwise operation.

WF uses classes in the `System.CodeDom.Compiler` namespace to dynamically generate and compile source code from the `CodeDom` object graph built from XAML. Once the runtime compiles the expression, WF can evaluate the rule to inspect its result.

Available Expressions

The small pieces of code we write for conditions are valid C# and VB.NET expressions. The expressions must evaluate to a Boolean value to be valid. For instance, all of the following expressions are valid. We can invoke methods, retrieve properties, index into arrays, and even use other classes from the base class library, like the `Regex` class for regular expressions.

```
this.x + 1 < 100
this.name.StartsWith("Scott")
Regex.Match(this.AreaCode, @"^\\(\\d{3}\\)\\s\\d{3}-\\d{4}$").Success
this.CheckIndex()
this.GetResult() != 10
this.numbers[this.x] == this.numbers[this.x + 1]
```

Expressions must evaluate to true or false. The following examples are invalid:

```
Console.Write(this.name)
this.x = this.GetResult()
```

Rules and Activation

In Chapter 2, we discussed workflow activation. Activation allows us to pass a XAML definition of our workflow to the workflow runtime, instead of using a compiled workflow definition. For instance, let's assume we have the following workflow definition in a file named `Activation.xoml`.

```
<SequentialWorkflowActivity
    xmlns="http://schemas.microsoft.com/winfx/2006/xaml/workflow">
    <WhileActivity>
        <WhileActivity.Condition>
            <RuleConditionReference ConditionName="Condition1" />
        </WhileActivity.Condition>
    <DelayActivity />
    </WhileActivity>
</SequentialWorkflowActivity>
```

Let's also assume our condition (Condition1) is in a file named Activation.rules. We can load the workflow and the rules file with the following code:

```
XmlReader definitionReader;
definitionReader = XmlReader.Create(@"..\..\conditions\Activation.
xoml");

XmlReader rulesReader;
rulesReader = XmlReader.Create(@"..\..\conditions\Activation.rules");

Dictionary<string, object> parameters = null;
WorkflowInstance instance;
instance = workflowRuntime.CreateWorkflow(
                    definitionReader, rulesReader, parameters
                );
```

Activation gives us a great deal of flexibility. For instance, we could store workflow and rule definitions inside database records, and update the rules without recompiling or redeploying an application.

The Conditioned Activity Group

Before we finish talking about conditions, we need to take a closer look at one condition-centric activity that is flexible and powerful. The ConditionedActivityGroup (CAG) executes a collection of child activities based on a WhenCondition attached to each child. Furthermore, the CAG continues to execute until an UntilCondition on the CAG returns true. This behavior makes the CAG somewhat of a cross between a While activity and a Parallel activity.

When we drop the CAG into the workflow designer, it will appear as shown in the screenshot overleaf. In the top of the activity shape is an activity storyboard where we can drop activities. The arrows on either side of the storyboard allow us to scroll through the child activities in the storyboard. When we select an activity in the storyboard, the selected activity will appear in the bottom of the activity shape inside the preview box. We can toggle between preview and edit modes using the button in the middle of the CAG's shape.

In the following screenshot, we've arranged some activities in the CAG's storyboard. The first activity is a Sequence activity, and we've selected the activity for editing. The bottom of the CAG's shape displays the Sequence activity in detail. Inside the Sequence activity, we have placed two Code activities.

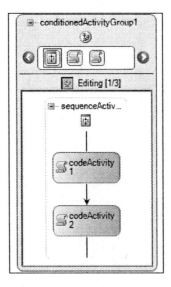

Since the Sequence activity is a direct descendant of the CAG, we can assign the Sequence activity a WhenCondition (see the screenshot on the next page). As with all conditions, the WhenCondition can be a code condition, or a declarative rule.

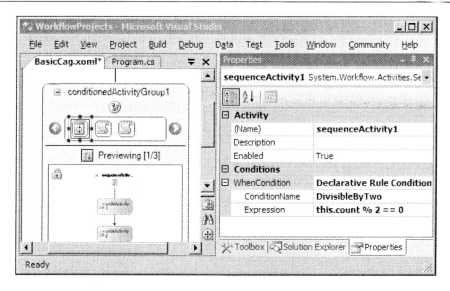

The CAG only executes a child activity if the WhenCondition returns true; however, the WhenCondition is optional. If we do not specify a WhenCondition, the child activity will execute only once. No matter how many times the CAG continues to loop, an activity without a WhenCondition will execute only during the first iteration.

The CAG repeatedly executes child activities until one of two things happens. First, the CAG itself has an UntilCondition (see the screenshot below). When the UntilCondition returns true, the CAG immediately stops processing and also cancels any currently executing child activities. Secondly, the CAG will stop processing if there are no child activities to execute. This can occur when the WhenConditions of all child activities return false.

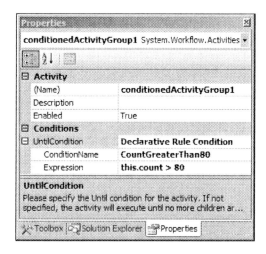

It's important to note that the CAG evaluates the `UntilCondition` when it first begins executing. If the condition returns true at this point, no child activities will execute. Also, the CAG evaluates the `UntilCondition` each time a child activity finishes execution. This means only a subset of the child activities may execute. Finally, the CAG doesn't guarantee the execution order of child activities, which is why the CAG is similar to the `Parallel` activity. For example, dropping a `Delay` activity inside the CAG will not block the CAG from executing its other child activities.

When to Use the CAG

The CAG is useful in goal-seeking scenarios. Let's say we are building a workflow to book flight, hotel, and car reservations for a trip. Inside the workflow, we might use web service activities to request pricing information from third-party systems. We can arrange the web service calls inside a CAG to request prices repeatedly until we meet a goal. Our goal might be for the total price of the trip to meet a minimum cost, or we might use a more advanced goal that includes cost, total travel time, and hotel class.

Working with Rules

The declarative rule conditions we've seen in the previous sections only return a value of true or false. A condition doesn't modify a workflow. A *rule*, on the other hand, is both a condition and a set of actions in an if-then-else form. The `Rule` class in Windows Workflow represents this if-then-else concept. The class diagram in the following screenshot displays classes with important relationships to the `Rule` class.

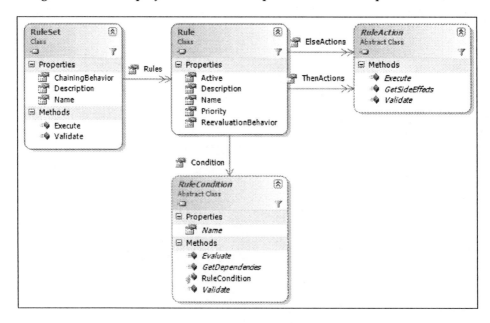

The first concept to notice is that the RuleSet class manages a collection of rules. The Policy activity will use the Execute method of a RuleSet to process the rule collection. We will cover the Policy activity in more detail soon.

Every Rule inside a RuleSet has a Condition property that references a single RuleCondition object. The RuleSet logic will use the Evaluate method of a RuleCondition to retrieve a value of true or false.

Every Rule maintains two collections of RuleAction objects—the ElseActions and the ThenActions. When a rule's condition evaluates to true, the runtime invokes the Execute method of each action in the ThenActions collection; otherwise the runtime invokes the Execute method of the actions in the ElseActions collection.

Now that we have a basic understanding of how rules work on the inside, let's take a look at the Policy activity.

The Policy Activity

The Encarta dictionary describes policy as a program of actions adopted by an individual, group, or government. Policies are everywhere in real life. Universities define policies for student admissions, and banks define policies for lending money. U.S. banks often base their lending policies on credit scores, and a credit score takes into account many variables, like an individual's age, record of past payment, income, and outstanding debt. Business policy can become very complex, and is full of declarative knowledge. As we discussed at the beginning of the chapter, declarative knowledge is about the relationships in data. For example, one bank's policy might say that if my credit score is less than 500 points, they will charge me an extra one percent in interest.

We also discussed in the beginning of the chapter how declarative knowledge is not well suited to general-purpose programming languages like C# and Visual Basic. Instead, specialized tools we call rules engines are best suited for managing and executing declarative knowledge. The Policy activity in Windows Workflow is one such rules engine.

Creating a Policy Workflow

Although we can use a Policy activity almost anywhere inside of a larger workflow, we will be using a simple workflow with only a single Policy activity inside. All we need is to create a new sequential workflow, and drag a Policy shape into the designer (see the screenshot overleaf).

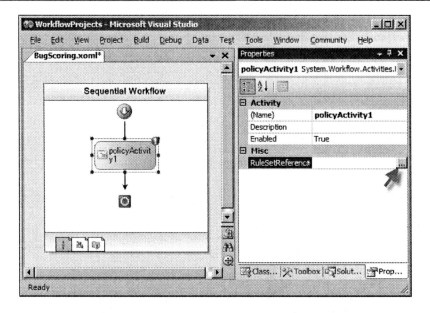

We can also see the **Properties** windows in the screenshot above. The
`RuleSetReference` property is the primary property of a `Policy` activity. We can
click the ellipsis button in the **Properties** window to launch the **Select Rule Set**
dialog box, shown in the screenshot below:

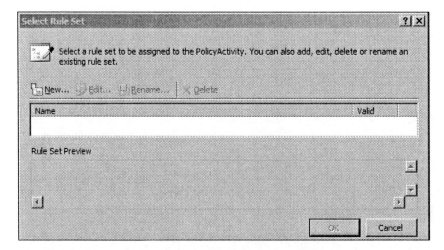

When we first create a workflow, we won't have any rule sets defined. A workflow
can contain multiple rule sets, and each rule set will contain one or more rules.
Although a `Policy` activity can only reference a single rule set, we might design a
workflow with multiple `Policy` activities inside, and need them each to reference a
different rule set.

Clicking on the **New** button in the dialog box will launch the **Rule Set Editor** dialog box as shown below:

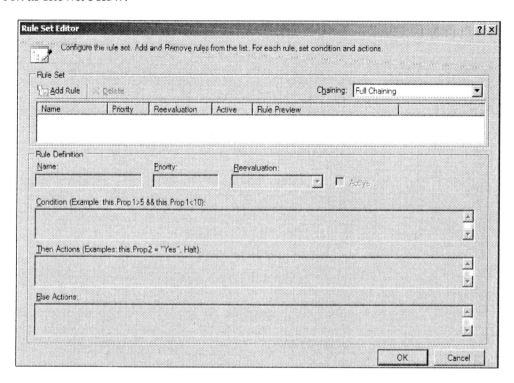

The **Rule Set Editor** exposes many options for rules and the rule set. For now, we are going to concentrate on conditions and actions. Let's suppose we are defining a policy to score a software bug. The score we compute will determine if we need to send notifications to team members who will need to take immediate action. The bug will be a member field in our workflow class, and will expose various properties (`Priority`, `IsOpenedByClient`) that we will inspect to compute a score. The `BugDetails` class listed below defines the bug:

```
public enum BugPriority
{
   Low,
   Medium,
   High
}
public class BugDetails
{
   private string _title;
   public string Title
   {
```

```
         get { return _title; }
         set { _title = value; }
      }
      private bool _openedByClient;
      public bool IsOpenedByClient
      {
         get { return _openedByClient; }
         set { _openedByClient = value; }
      }
      private bool _isSecurityRelated;
      public bool IsSecurityRelated
      {
         get { return _isSecurityRelated; }
         set { _isSecurityRelated = value; }
      }
      private bool _isVerified;
      public bool IsVerified
      {
         get { return _isVerified; }
         set { _isVerified = value; }
      }
      private BugPriority _priority;
      public BugPriority Priority
      {
         get { return _priority; }
         set { _priority = value; }
      }
      private int _score;
      public int Score
      {
         get { return _score; }
         set { _score = value; }
      }
   }
```

Our first three rules will determine a bug's base score by looking at the bug's priority setting. We can start by clicking the **Add Rule** button in the dialog box. Our first rule will have the condition of this.Bug.Priority == BugPriority.Low, and a Then action of this.Score = 0. In the dialog box, we can give this rule a meaningful name of SetScore_LowPriority.

The conditions in our rules are just like the conditions we examined earlier in the chapter. We can use tests for equality, inequality, greater than, or less than. We can call methods, and index into arrays. As long as the condition's expression returns a true or false, and can be represented by types in the `System.CodeDom` namespace, we will have a valid expression.

The actions in our rules have even greater flexibility. An action can also invoke methods and interact with fields and properties, but is not restricted to returning a Boolean value. In fact, most actions will perform assignments and manipulate fields and properties in a workflow. In the `SetScore_LowPriority` rule, we've used a rule action to assign an initial score of 0. Remember too that the action properties on rules are collections, meaning we can specify multiple actions for then and else. We will need to place each action on a separate line inside the action text box.

Our bug can take on one of three possible priority values (Low, Medium, or High), so we'll need a rule to set the bug score for each possible priority level. Once we've entered the three rules, the **Rule Set Editor** should look as shown in the following screenshot. Notice we have left the `Priority` and `Reevaluation` properties for each rule at their default values. We will return to cover these properties soon.

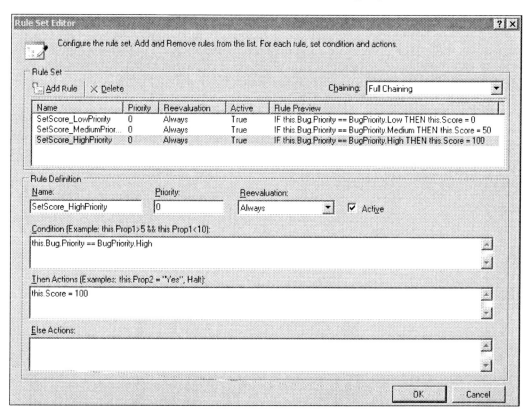

Evaluation

These rules, like the declarative conditions we used earlier, will live in a `.rules` file. When a rule set executes, it will process each rule by evaluating the rule's condition and executing the `then` or `else` actions. The rule set continues processing in this fashion until it has processed every rule in the rule set, or until it encounters a `Halt` instruction. `Halt` is a keyword we can place in a rule's action list that will stop the rule set from processing additional rules.

With these rules in place, we could execute our workflow and watch the `Policy` activity compute our bug score by executing the rule set we've defined. There is still an additional rule we would like to add to our rule set, however. The rule should say, "If the bug's score is greater than 75, then send an email to the development team". This rule presents a potential problem, however, since it would not work if the rule set evaluates this rule before evaluating the rules that assign the score. We need to make sure the score for a bug is set first, and we can achieve this goal using rule priorities.

Priority

Each rule has a `Priority` property of type `Int32`. We can see this property exposed in the **Rule Set Editor** as shown in the following screenshot. Before executing rules, the rule set will sort its rules into a list ordered by priority. A rule with a high priority value will execute before a rule with a low priority value. The rule with the highest priority in the rule set will execute first. Rules of equal priority will execute in the alphabetic order of their `Name` property.

To make sure our notification rule is evaluated last, we need to assign the rule a priority of 0, and ensure all other rules have a higher priority. In the following screenshot, we've given our first three rules a priority of 100. The number we use for priority is arbitrary, as it only controls the relative execution order. It is always a good idea to leave a gap between priority values so we can squeeze in more rules later on.

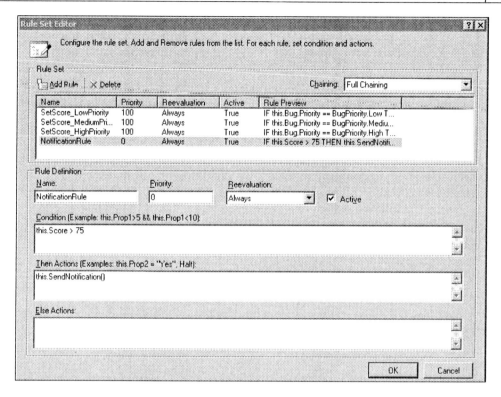

Rule Dependencies

All the rules we've written so far are independent. Our rules do not modify any fields in the workflow that other rules depend upon. Suppose, however, we had a rule that said:

"If the `IsSecurityRelated` property of the bug is true, set the bug `Priority` to High."

Obviously, this rule impacts on the `SetScore_HighPriority` rule that sets our bug score to 100 when the bug's `Priority` field is set to `High`.

One solution to this problem would be to set the relative priorities of the rules to ensure the `set score` rules always execute *after* any rule that might set the `Priority` field. However, this type of solution isn't always feasible as the rule set grows and the dependencies between the rules become more entangled.

Fortunately, Windows Workflow can simplify this scenario. If you look back at the class diagram in the screenshot under the section *Working with Rules*, you'll notice the `RuleCondition` class carries a `GetDependencies` method, and a `RuleAction` class carries a `GetSideEffects` method. These two methods allow the rules engine to match the *dependencies* of a rule (the fields and properties the rule's condition inspects to compute a value) against the *side effects* of other rules (the fields and properties a rule's action modifies). When an action produces a side effect that matches a dependency from a previously executed rule, the rules engine can go back and re-evaluate the previous rule. In rules engine terminology, we call this feature **forward chaining**. The chaining feature in Windows Workflow can work implicitly or explicitly.

Implicit Chaining

By default, the forward chaining in Windows Workflow is implicit. That is to say, Windows Workflow takes care of managing side effects, dependencies, and rule re-evaluation and we do not need to take any extra steps. The rules engine examines the expressions in each rule condition and each rule action to produce lists of dependencies and side effects. We can go ahead and write our rule as `AdjustBugPriorityForSecurity`, as shown below:

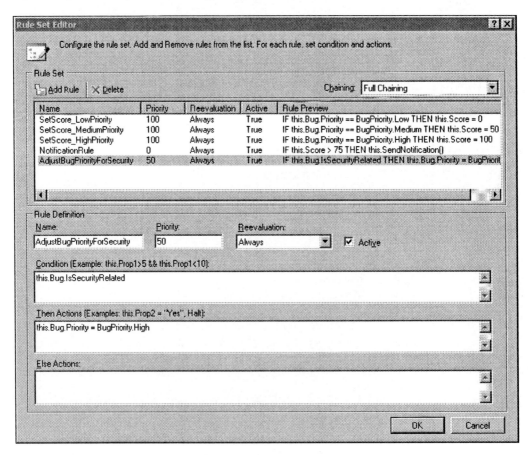

Now, if the workflow looks at a bug with the `IsSecurityRelated` property set to true, the action of the new rule will change the bug's `Priority` to `High`. The full rule looks like the following:

```
IF this.Bug.IsSecurityRelated
THEN this.Bug.Priority = BugPriority.High
```

The rules engine will know that three previous rules have a dependency on the `Priority` property and re-evaluate all three rules. All of this happens before the `NotificationRule` runs, so a bug with `IsSecurityRelated` set will create a score of 100, and the `NotificationRule` will invoke the `SendNotification` method.

Implicit chaining is a great feature because we don't have to calculate dependencies manually. For implicit chaining to work, however, the rules engine must be able to infer the dependencies by parsing the rule expression. If we have a rule that calls into our compiled code, or into third-party code, the rules engine can no longer resolve the dependencies. In these scenarios, we can take advantage of chaining using metadata attributes or explicit actions.

Chaining with Attributes

Let's suppose the logic we need to execute for a rule is complicated—so complicated we don't feel comfortable writing all the logic declaratively. What we can do is place the logic inside a method in our code-behind file, and invoke the method from our rule. As an example, let's write the last rule like the following:

```
IF this.Bug.IsSecurityRelated
THEN this.AdjustBugForSecurity()
```

As we mentioned, this method call presents a problem if we need forward chaining. The rules engine will not know which fields and properties the `AdjustBugForSecurity` method will change. The good news is that Windows Workflow provides attributes we can use to declare a method's dependencies and side effects.

Attribute	Description
RuleWrite	Declares a field or property that the method will change (a side effect of the method).
RuleRead	Declares a field or property that the method will read (a dependency of the method).
RuleInvoke	Declares a method that the current method will invoke. The engine will inspect the second method for additional attributes.

If a method does not carry one of the above attributes, the rules engine will assume the method does not read or write any fields or properties. If we want forward chaining to work with our method, we'll need to define it as follows:

```
[RuleWrite("Bug/Priority")]
public void AdjustBugForSecurity()
{
   // .. other work
   Bug.Priority = BugPriority.High;
   // .. other work
}
```

The `RuleWrite` attribute uses a syntax similar to the property binding syntax in Windows Workflow. This particular `RuleWrite` attribute declares that the method will write to the `Priority` property of the `Bug` class. The rules engine can also parse a wildcard syntax, so that `[RuleWrite("Bug/*")]` would tell the engine that the method writes to *all* the fields and properties on the bug object. The `RuleRead` attribute uses the same syntax, except we would use this attribute on methods called from the conditional part of our rules, to tell the engine about dependencies of the method.

We can use the `RuleInvoke` attribute when our method calls into other methods, as shown in the following example:

```
[RuleInvoke("SetBugPriorityHigh")]
public void AdjustBugForSecurity()
{
   // .. other work
   SetBugPriorityHigh();
   // .. other work
}
[RuleWrite("Bug/Priority")]
void SetBugPriorityHigh()
{
   Bug.Priority = BugPriority.High;
}
```

In this code sample we've told the rules engine that the method called from our rule will in turn call the `SetBugPriorityHigh` method. The rules engine will inspect the `SetBugPriorityHigh` method and find a `RuleWrite` attribute that will preserve forward chaining.

Explicit Chaining

In some scenarios, we may need to call into third-party code from our rules. This third-party code may have side effects, but since we do not own the code, we cannot add a `RuleWrite` attribute. In this scenario, we can use an explicit `Update` statement in our rule actions. For example, if we used an explicit `Update` statement with our `AdjustBugForSecurity` method instead of the `RuleWrite` attribute, we'd write our declarative rule condition like the following:

```
this.AdjustBugForSecurity()
Update("this/Bug/Priority/")
```

Note that the update statement syntax is again similar to our `RuleWrite` syntax, and that there is no corresponding `Read` statement available. It is generally better to use the attribute-based approach whenever possible. This explicit approach is designed for scenarios when we cannot add method attributes, or when we need precise control over the chaining behavior, which is discussed in the following section on *Chaining Behavior*.

Controlling Chaining

The forward chaining behavior of the rule set is powerful. We can execute rules and have them re-evaluated even when we don't know their interdependencies. However, there can be times when chaining can produce unpleasant results. For instance, it is possible to put the rules engine into an infinite loop. It is also possible that we will write a rule that we do not want the engine to re-evaluate. Fortunately, there are several options available to tweak rule processing.

Chaining Behavior

The first option is a `ChainingBehavior` property on the `RuleSet` class. The **Rule Set Editor** exposes this property with a drop-down list labeled **Chaining**. The available options are **Sequential**, **Explicit Update Only**, and **Full Chaining**. **Full Chaining** is the default rule set behavior, and provides us with the forward chaining rule evaluation we've described so far.

The **Explicit Update Only** option tells the rules engine not to use implicit chaining. In addition, the rules engine will ignore `RuleWrite` and `RuleRead` attributes. With **Explicit Update Only** selected, the only mechanism that will trigger rule re-evaluation is with the explicit `Update` statement we described in the last section. Explicit updates give us precise control over the rules that can cause a re-evaluation of previous rules.

The **Sequential** option disables chaining altogether. A rule set operating with sequential behavior will execute all its rules only once, and in the order specified by their respective `Priority` properties (of course, a `Halt` statement could still terminate the rule processing before all rules complete execution).

Re-evaluation Behavior

Another option to control chaining is to use the `ReevaluationBehavior` property of a rule. This property is exposed in the **Rule Set** editor by a drop-down list labeled **Reevaluation**. The available options are **Always** and **Never**.

Always is the default behavior for a rule. The rules engine will always re-evaluate a rule with this setting, if the proper criteria are met. This setting would not override a rule set chaining behavior of `Sequential`, for instance.

Never, as the name implies, turns off re-evaluation. It is important to know that the rules engine only considers a rule `evaluated` if the rule executes a non-empty action. For example, consider a rule that has `Then` actions, but no `Else` actions, like the rules we've defined. If the rule is evaluated and its condition returns false, the rule is still a candidate for re-evaluation because the rule has not executed any actions.

Rules Engine Tracing and Tracking

Given the various chaining behaviors, and the complexities of some real-world rule sets, we will find it useful to see what is happening inside the rules engine. As we discussed in Chapter 6, Windows Workflow takes advantage of the .NET 2.0 tracing API and its own built-in tracking features to supply instrumentation information. In this section, we will explore the tracing and tracking features of the rules engine. Refer to Chapter 6 for general details on tracing and tracking.

Tracing Rules

To set up tracing for the rules engine we need an application configuration file with some trace switches set. The following configuration file will log all trace information from the rules engine to a `WorkflowTrace.log` file. The file will appear in the application's working directory.

```xml
<?xml version="1.0" encoding="utf-8" ?>
<configuration>
    <system.diagnostics>
      <switches>
        <add name="System.Workflow.Activities.Rules" value="All" />
        <add name="System.Workflow LogToFile" value="1" />
      </switches>
    </system.diagnostics>
</configuration>
```

The amount of detail provided by the trace information can be useful for tracking down chaining and logic problems in our rule sets. The rule set we've been working with in this chapter will produce the following trace information (some trace information is omitted for the sake of brevity).

```
Rule "SetScore_HighPriority" Condition dependency: "this/Bug/Priority/"
Rule "SetScore_HighPriority" THEN side-effect: "this/Score/"
Rule "SetScore_LowPriority" Condition dependency: "this/Bug/Priority/"
Rule "SetScore_LowPriority" THEN side-effect: "this/Score/"
Rule "SetScore_MediumPriority" Condition dependency:
                                        "this/Bug/Priority/"
Rule "SetScore_MediumPriority" THEN side-effect: "this/Score/"
Rule "AdjustBugForSecurity" Condition dependency:
                                        "this/Bug/IsSecurityRelated/"
Rule "AdjustBugForSecurity" THEN side-effect: "this/Bug/Priority/"
Rule "NotificationRule" Condition dependency: "this/Score/"
Rule "SetScore_HighPriority" THEN actions trigger rule
                                        "NotificationRule"
Rule "SetScore_LowPriority" THEN actions trigger rule
                                        "NotificationRule"
Rule "SetScore_MediumPriority" THEN actions trigger rule
                                        "NotificationRule"
Rule "AdjustBugForSecurity" THEN actions trigger rule
                                        "SetScore_HighPriority"
Rule "AdjustBugForSecurity" THEN actions trigger rule
                                        "SetScore_LowPriority"
Rule "AdjustBugForSecurity" THEN actions trigger rule
                                        "SetScore_MediumPriority"
```

This first part of the trace will provide information about dependency and side effect analysis. By the end of the analysis, we can see which actions will trigger the re-evaluation of other rules. Later in the trace, we can observe each step the rule engine takes when executing our rule set.

```
Rule Set "BugScoring": Executing
Evaluating condition on rule "SetScore_HighPriority".
Rule "SetScore_HighPriority" condition evaluated to False.
Evaluating condition on rule "SetScore_LowPriority".
Rule "SetScore_LowPriority" condition evaluated to False.
Evaluating condition on rule "SetScore_MediumPriority".
Rule "SetScore_MediumPriority" condition evaluated to True.
Evaluating THEN actions for rule "SetScore_MediumPriority".
Evaluating condition on rule "AdjustBugForSecurity".
Rule "AdjustBugForSecurity" condition evaluated to True.
Evaluating THEN actions for rule "AdjustBugForSecurity".
Rule "AdjustBugForSecurity" side effects enable rule
```

```
                      "SetScore_HighPriority" reevaluation.
        Rule "AdjustBugForSecurity" side effects enable rule
                      "SetScore_LowPriority" reevaluation.
        Rule "AdjustBugForSecurity" side effects enable rule
                      "SetScore_MediumPriority" reevaluation.
        Evaluating condition on rule "SetScore_HighPriority".
        Rule "SetScore_HighPriority" condition evaluated to True.
        Evaluating THEN actions for rule "SetScore_HighPriority".
        Evaluating condition on rule "SetScore_LowPriority".
        Rule "SetScore_LowPriority" condition evaluated to False.
        Evaluating condition on rule "SetScore_MediumPriority".
        Rule "SetScore_MediumPriority" condition evaluated to False.
        Evaluating condition on rule "NotificationRule".
        Rule "NotificationRule" condition evaluated to True.
        Evaluating THEN actions for rule "NotificationRule".
```

There is a tremendous amount of detail in the trace. We can see the result of each condition evaluation, and which rules the engine re-evaluates due to side effects. These facts can prove invaluable when debugging a misbehaving rule set.

A more formal mechanism to capture this information is to use a tracking service, which we cover in the next section. Although the tracking information is not as detailed as the trace information, tracking is designed to record information in production applications while tracing is geared for debugging.

Tracking Rules

As discussed in Chapter 6, WF provides extensible and scalable tracking features to monitor workflow execution. One tracking service WF provides is a SQL Server tracking service that records events to a SQL Server table. The default tracking profile for this service records all workflow events.

To enable tracking, we'll need a tracking schema installed in SQL Server, and an application configuration file to configure tracking. The following configuration file will add the tracking service to the WF runtime and point to a WorkflowDB database on the local machine.

```xml
<?xml version="1.0" encoding="utf-8" ?>
<configuration>

  <configSections>
    <section
      name="WorkflowWithTracking"
      type="System.Workflow.Runtime.Configuration.
            WorkflowRuntimeSection,
            System.Workflow.Runtime, Version=3.0.00000.0,
```

```
                    Culture=neutral, PublicKeyToken=31bf3856ad364e35"/>
        </configSections>

    <WorkflowWithTracking>
      <CommonParameters>
        <add name-"ConnectionString"
             value="Data Source=(local);Initial Catalog=WorkflowDB;
                                      Integrated Security=true"/>
      </CommonParameters>
      <Services>
        <add
          type="System.Workflow.Runtime.Tracking.SqlTrackingService,
                System.Workflow.Runtime, Version=3.0.00000.0,
                Culture=neutral, PublicKeyToken=31bf3856ad364e35"/>
      </Services>
    </WorkflowWithTracking>

  </configuration>
```

If we run our bug scoring workflow with the above tracking, we can pull out rule-related tracking information. The following code uses the instance ID of the completed workflow as a lookup key to retrieve the tracking information from the SQL database into which the information has already been persisted. We do not need to modify the workflow itself to use tracking.

```csharp
private static void DumpRuleTrackingEvents(Guid instanceId)
{
  WorkflowRuntimeSection config;
  config = ConfigurationManager.GetSection("WorkflowWithTracking")
           as WorkflowRuntimeSection;

  SqlTrackingQuery sqlTrackingQuery = new SqlTrackingQuery();
  sqlTrackingQuery.ConnectionString =
     config.CommonParameters["ConnectionString"].Value;

  SqlTrackingWorkflowInstance sqlTrackingWorkflowInstance;

  if (sqlTrackingQuery.TryGetWorkflow(
            instanceId, out sqlTrackingWorkflowInstance))
  {
    Console.WriteLine("{0,-10} {1,-22} {2,-17}",
                      "Time", "Rule", "Condition Result");

    foreach (UserTrackingRecord userTrackingRecord in
            sqlTrackingWorkflowInstance.UserEvents)
    {
      RuleActionTrackingEvent ruleActionTrackingEvent =
        userTrackingRecord.UserData as RuleActionTrackingEvent;
```

```
        if (ruleActionTrackingEvent != null)
        {
            Console.WriteLine("{0,-12} {1,-25} {2,-17}",
            userTrackingRecord.EventDateTime.ToShortTimeString(),
            ruleActionTrackingEvent.RuleName.ToString(),
            ruleActionTrackingEvent.ConditionResult.ToString());
        }
    }
  }
}
```

Notice that to retrieve the rule-tracking events we need to dig into the user data associated with a `UserTrackingRecord`. The above code will produce the following output, which includes the result of each rule evaluation.

Dynamic Updates

Earlier, we mentioned that one of the advantages to using declarative rules is that we can dynamically modify rules and rule sets at run time. If these rules were specified in code, we'd have to recompile and redeploy the application each time we wanted to modify any rule sets. With WF, we can use the `WorkflowChanges` class to alter an instance of a workflow.

If we give the following code an instance of our bug-scoring workflow, it will initialize a new `WorkflowChanges` object with our workflow definition. We can then find the bug-scoring rule set by name via a `RuleDefinitions` instance. Once we have our rule set, we can make changes to our rules.

```
private static void ModifyWorkflow(WorkflowInstance instance)
{
    Activity workflowDefinition = instance.GetWorkflowDefinition();

    WorkflowChanges workflowchanges;

    workflowchanges = new WorkflowChanges(workflowDefinition);

    CompositeActivity transient = workflowchanges.TransientWorkflow;

    RuleDefinitions ruleDefinitions =
```

```
    (RuleDefinitions)transient.GetValue(
        RuleDefinitions.RuleDefinitionsProperty
    );
RuleSet ruleSet = ruleDefinitions.RuleSets["BugScoring"];
foreach (Rule rule in ruleSet.Rules)
{
    if (rule.Name == "AdjustBugPriorityForSecurity")
    {
        rule.Active = false;
    }
    if (rule.Name == "NotificationRule")
    {
        RuleExpressionCondition condition;
        condition = rule.Condition as RuleExpressionCondition;
        CodeBinaryOperatorExpression expression;
        expression = condition.Expression as
                        CodeBinaryOperatorExpression;
        expression.Right = new CodePrimitiveExpression(120);
    }
}
instance.ApplyWorkflowChanges(workflowchanges);
}
```

Once we have our rule set, we can iterate through our rules. In the above code, we are turning off the `AdjustBugPriorityForSecurity` rule. We can enable and disable rules on the fly by toggling the `Active` property of a rule.

The modifications the code makes will apply to one specific instance of a workflow. In other words, we aren't changing the compiled workflow definition. If we wanted to turn the security rule off for all workflows in the future, we'd either have to run this code on every bug scoring workflow we create, or modify the rule set in the designer and recompile.

In addition, the above code makes changes that are even more dramatic to our notification rule. We are changing the rule's conditional expression from `this.score > 75` to `this.score > 120`. Expressions can be tricky to manipulate, but remember the `.rules` file will contain an XML representation of the `CodeDom` objects that make the rule. We can look inside the file to see how the condition is built for the `NotificationRule` (shown overleaf).

```
<RuleExpressionCondition.Expression>
  <ns0:CodeBinaryOperatorExpression Operator="GreaterThan">
    <ns0:CodeBinaryOperatorExpression.Left>
      <ns0:CodePropertyReferenceExpression PropertyName="Score">
        <ns0:CodePropertyReferenceExpression.TargetObject>
          <ns0:CodeThisReferenceExpression />
        </ns0:CodePropertyReferenceExpression.TargetObject>
      </ns0:CodePropertyReferenceExpression>
    </ns0:CodeBinaryOperatorExpression.Left>
    <ns0:CodeBinaryOperatorExpression.Right>
      <ns0:CodePrimitiveExpression>
        <ns0:CodePrimitiveExpression.Value>
          <ns1:Int32 >75</ns1:Int32>
        </ns0:CodePrimitiveExpression.Value>
      </ns0:CodePrimitiveExpression>
    </ns0:CodeBinaryOperatorExpression.Right>
  </ns0:CodeBinaryOperatorExpression>
</RuleExpressionCondition.Expression>
</RuleExpressionCondition>
```

Looking at the XML we can see that we need to replace the
CodePrimitiveExpression assigned to the Right property of the
CodeBinaryOperatorExpression. Using the CodeDom types we could replace the
condition, modify actions, and even build new rules on the fly.

Summary

In this chapter, we've covered conditions and rules in Windows Workflow. There
are several activities in WF featuring conditional logic, including the powerful
ConditionedActivityGroup. The purpose of the Windows Workflow Policy
activity is to execute sets of rules. These rules contain declarative knowledge, and
we can prioritize rules and use forward chaining execution semantics. By writing
out our business knowledge in declarative statements instead of in procedural code,
we gain a great deal of flexibility. We can track and trace rules, and update rule sets
dynamically. Windows Workflow is a capable rules engine.

Index

C

CAG. *See* **conditioned activity group**
conditioned activity group
  about 211
  activities 212
  in workflow designer 211-214
  using 214
conditions
  .rules file, rule conditions 208, 209
  about 204
  available expressions, rule conditions 210
  code conditions 205-207
  conditioned activity group 211-214
  conditioned activity group, using 214
  rule conditions 207-211
  rules and activation, rule conditions
    210, 211
  working with 205
correlation parameters
  about 180-182
  correlation alias, correlation attributes 184
  correlation attributes 183, 184
  correlation initializer, correlation attributes
    184
  correlation parameter, correlation attributes
    184
  correlation tokens, correlation attributes
    185, 186
  derivation 116
custom activities
  activity composition 103-111
  activity composition, reusability 102
  activity execution 122-127
  building 103
  dependency properties 111-116
  domain specific languages 102, 103
  extensibility 102
  need for 101-103
  reusability 102

D

declarative knowledge 203
dependency properties
  about 111-113
  activity binding 113

  attached properties 114
  meta properties 115
derivation
  about 116
  activity components 119-122
  activity designers, activity components
    120-122
  activity validators, activity components 119
  ConsoleWriteActivity 117, 118

L

local communication services
  authorization, role-based 186-188
  correlation parameters 180-186
  redux 179, 180
  workflow queues 189-193

P

persistence services 139
policy
  about 215
  chaining behavior, controlling chaining 225
  chaining with attributes, rule dependencies
    223, 224
  controlling chaining 225
  evaluation 220
  explicit chaining, rule dependencies 225
  forward chaining, rule dependencies 222
  implicit chaining, rule dependencies 222,
    223
  priority 220
  re-evaluation behavior, controlling chain-
    ing 226
  rule dependencies 221-224
  workflow, creating 215-218
procedural knowledge 203
pure code approach
  about 27
  with Visual Studio 28-30
pure XAML approach
  about 32, 33
  code generation 42-44
  custom activities, using 35, 36
  workflows, compiling 36-44
  workflows, compiling with MSBuild 40-42

workflows, compiling with Wfc.exe 37, 38
workflows, compiling with
    WorkflowCompiler 38, 39
XAML, activating 45
XAML serialization 42-44

R

rules
  about 204
  dynamic updates 230-232
  policy activity 215
  rules engine 226-229
  tracing rules, rules engine 226-228
  tracking rules, rules engine 228, 229
  working with 214
runtime, Windows Workflow
  configuring 133, 134
  environment, managing 130
  events 130
  logging 131
  trace listener 132
  trace sources, enabling 131
  workflow configuration sections 133
  WorkflowRuntime class 129
  workflows, managing 130

S

scheduling services
  about 135
  configuration 137, 138
  criteria for choosing 139
  scheduling parameters 139
  threads 135, 136
sequential workflow
  companion property, parameters 61
  events 56-60
  events, raising 62-70
  events and methods 62
  fault handlers 70-72
  fault handlers, configuring 72
  host implementation, events and methods
      69, 70
  methods, invoking 62-70
  parameters 60-62
  SequenceActivity 51, 52

sequence inside sequence, SequenceActivity
    54-56
service contracts, events and methods 63-65
service implementation, events and
    methods 65, 66
simple flow, SequenceActivity 52, 53
tracking service for workflow monitoring
    60
workflow implementation, events and
    methods 66-68
state machine
  about 161
  bugs 165-167
  completed state, state activity 167
  driving 171, 172
  event 162
  event driven activity, state activity 168, 169
  first state machine 163-172
  hierarchical state machines 176, 177
  initial state, state activity 167
  inspecting 173-175
  in Windows Workflow 162
  project, creating 163-165
  SetState activity, state activity 169-171
  state 162
  state activity 167-171
  StateFinalization activity, state activity 171
  StateInitialization activity, state activity 171
  state machine workflow 161
  transition 162

V

Visual Studio 2005 Extensions
  about 12, 13
  designer looks 15
  validation & debugging 15
  XAML 13, 14

W

web service communication
  InvokeWebService activity 201, 202
  WebServiceInput activity 195
  WebServiceOutput activity 196, 197
  web service workflows, publishing 197-199
  workflows as web service clients 200-202

workflows as web services 194-198

Windows Workflow

.NET 3.0 framework, downloading 19

activities 11, 12

base activity library 75

basic activities 75-83

code and XAML together 47, 48

compensation activities 90-92

compiling workflows, pure XAML
    approach 36-44

conditions and rules activities 92-94

correlation parameters 180-186

custom activities 11, 12, 101

custom activities, pure XAML approach
    35, 36

debugging feature, Visual Studio 2005
    Extensions 15

designer looks, Visual Studio 2005
    Extensions 15

event driven workflow 51

execution styles 51

fault handling activities 87-89

first workflow, creating 19-24

local communication events, activities
    84-87

local communication services 179

local communication services, redux 179

objects and their relationships 31

persistence services 139

persistence services, runtime services 18

pure code and Visual Studio 28-31

pure code approach 27-31

pure XAML approach 32-45

runtime 15-19, 129-134

runtime, configuring 133, 134

runtime, hosting 16, 17

runtime events 130

runtime logging 131-133

runtime services 17

scheduling services 135-139

scheduling services, runtime services 18

sequential workflow 51

state activities 96-100

trace listener, runtime 132, 133

trace sources, runtime 131

tracking services, runtime services 19

transaction activities 89, 90

transaction services, runtime services 18

validation, Visual Studio 2005 Extensions
    15

Visual Studio 2005 Extensions 12-15

Visual Studio 2005 Extensions,
    downloading 19

web service communication 194

web services activities 95, 96

XAML, Visual Studio 2005 Extensions 13,
    14

XAML activation, pure XAML approach 45

Windows Workflow runtime

about 15

hosting 16

services 17-19

workflow

approach 27

declarative style, approach 27

imperative style, approach 27

workflow, compiling

code generation 42-44

with MSBuild 40-42

with Wfc.exe 37, 38

with workflow compiler 38-40

XAML serialization 42-44

workflow queues

about 189

queues, communicating with 194

waiting activity, cancelling 193

waiting activity, finding 191-193

WorkflowQueue 190

WorkflowQueueInfo 190

PUBLISHING

**Thank you for buying
Programming Windows Workflow
Foundation: Practical WF Techniques
and Examples using XAML and C#**

About Packt Publishing

Packt, pronounced 'packed', published its first book "*Mastering phpMyAdmin for Effective MySQL Management*" in April 2004 and subsequently continued to specialize in publishing highly focused books on specific technologies and solutions.

Our books and publications share the experiences of your fellow IT professionals in adapting and customizing today's systems, applications, and frameworks. Our solution based books give you the knowledge and power to customize the software and technologies you're using to get the job done. Packt books are more specific and less general than the IT books you have seen in the past. Our unique business model allows us to bring you more focused information, giving you more of what you need to know, and less of what you don't.

Packt is a modern, yet unique publishing company, which focuses on producing quality, cutting-edge books for communities of developers, administrators, and newbies alike. For more information, please visit our website: www.packtpub.com.

Writing for Packt

We welcome all inquiries from people who are interested in authoring. Book proposals should be sent to authors@packtpub.com. If your book idea is still at an early stage and you would like to discuss it first before writing a formal book proposal, contact us; one of our commissioning editors will get in touch with you.

We're not just looking for published authors; if you have strong technical skills but no writing experience, our experienced editors can help you develop a writing career, or simply get some additional reward for your expertise.

Printed in the United Kingdom
by Lightning Source UK Ltd.
118077UK00001B/113-130